Walking in the Covenant of Salt

Ron Miller

INTRODUCTION

For years I have been preaching and teaching about the covenant of salt. I am persuaded that now is the right timing for this book. Though the term *The Covenant of Salt* or *The Salt of the Covenant* appears only three times in the Scripture, this powerful covenant is found throughout the Old and New Testaments. Perhaps the limited use of the term in Scripture contributes to the fact that it is for the most part unheard of by the church. The pages of this book are dedicated to the illumination of this covenant to the believer. Therefore, we will linger mostly in and around the wonderful Biblical truths set forth therein.

After years of walking in the covenant, I am deeply persuaded of its power and fruitfulness. Actually, every true move of God has embraced its components. People who have never become acquainted Biblically with the salt covenant have been led into it by the precious Holy Spirit and tasted the wonderful benefits of it. Anywhere I speak on the subject, people will say to me afterwards, "That's what I have and that's what I walk in, but I didn't know what to call it."

Sometimes people will say that the understanding of this covenant has made them hungry to go very deep in their walk with the Lord.

I am on a much more urgent mission than just to be a blessing to the church, although I hope this book is that, too. I believe that it is time for the remnant church to rise from its anemic condition and walk in the last day glory that accompanies the latter rain of the church age. Every honest praying saint will bear witness that the church must have a radical change in order for the latter rain to be more than the former rain, which is God's pattern.

Saints around the world are anticipating a wave of Pentecost that will out-Pentecost Pentecost. Intercession is intense, and many are weeping between the porch and the altar, crying and groaning for the manifestation of His last day glory. They will not be denied. Their supplication and confession is one voice blended together with the request of Moses, "Let me see your glory," and the tenacious statement of Jacob, "I will not let you go until you bless me."

The air for revival is getting thick. The remnant church is pregnant with this child, and it is soon to be delivered. I firmly believe that the Lord will not do this mighty work outside of His covenants, and the covenant of salt will play a very important part in the last day move. It is out of this firm belief that I have received the unction to write the following pages.

We have heard of the blood covenant. We have heard of the Abrahamic covenant. We know how to transfer the blood covenant and the Abrahamic covenant from the old covenant to the new covenant priesthood. Now it is time for the salt covenant. The blood covenant is redemption. The Abrahamic covenant is riches. The salt covenant is responsibility. The blood covenant is protection. The Abrahamic covenant is prosperity. The salt covenant is productivity. I am not minimizing these wonderful familiar covenants in order to maximize another, but I am exhorting on a covenant that has somehow gone much too unnoticed. The believer must be balanced and perfected to the glory of the Lord Jesus. This takes *"The Salt of the New Covenant."*

The Bible makes it very clear that the Lord's glory falls only on a covenant people. Abraham was covenant; Lot was not. Isaac was covenant; Ishmael was not. Jacob was covenant; Esau was not. God's covenant people were safe in the land of Goshen, while Egypt encountered the anathema of God. Samuel was covenant, but Eli slid backwards from the covenant. Zadok was covenant; Abiathar was not. Abijah saw the glory fall because he was in the covenant. Jeroboam saw the wrath of God because he was not. John the Baptist walked in the covenant and was the real high priest of Israel; while Ciaiphas, the elected high priest, was not.

The Lord's true church must walk in the power of the covenants as a called out assembly, a kingdom of priests walking in the new covenant priesthood of the believer. When the priesthood of God walks therein, the devil will have his hands full. The scoffers and the skeptics will shut their mouths. The world will see the light, and the church will see the glory of the Lord fill the whole earth. Let us explore this Bible covenant exhaustively and embrace it as energetically as any other Bible covenant.

A NOTE FROM THE AUTHOR

I firmly believe that the true test of a Christian book is whether or not it drives the reader to the Scriptures. If a Christian book competes with the Bible for your attention, there is something wrong. If it does not give you hunger pangs for the Word of God, it is better not to read it. This has been the standard I have used for years. I believe it is a hard, but true test. It is only fitting that I should give account of myself and the hard test that I have so easily placed on other writings.

I am now writing my first book and nearly tremble to think it would fail this test. God forbid that the following pages would fail to burn the heart of the sincere believer with a heavenly desire to devour the truths of God's infallible Word. God forbid that anybody would be exalted but the Lord Jesus Christ.

There are many wonderful men and women of God that have greatly helped in this endeavor, without whom the book could not have been completed. Their tremendous influence and effort have not gone unnoticed.

CONTENTS

CHAPTER ONE

THE CONTENTS OF THE COVENANT OF SALT

In order to understand the covenants of the Lord, we must follow the pattern given unto us. In Ephesians 2:12, we find these words: *"That at that time ye were without Christ, being aliens from the Commonwealth of Israel and strangers from the covenants of promise, having no hope, and without God in the world."* We were dead in trespasses and sin. We were strangers from the covenants. We must conclude that the covenants are for the children of God. These covenants come to all people through the Commonwealth of Israel and by the blood of Jesus. This is the pattern to receive the covenants. They are first given to the Jews, and then made available to all men through Jesus.

> *The covenants of God given to Israel are made available to all men through Jesus.*

The following verse in Chapter 2 of Ephesians tells

us, *"But now in Christ Jesus ye who were sometimes far off are made nigh by the blood of Christ."* The redeemed of the Lord, washed in the blood, regenerated children of God have access to the covenants that were once given to the children of Abraham. Now we are not to be strangers to those covenants of Israel, for we have been grafted in by the precious blood of Jesus. Therefore, we will look at the contents of the covenant of salt delivered first to the children of Israel, and then we will be able to see clearly how all saints can embrace it properly. Instead of being a stranger to this covenant, we are going to walk in it.

The first mention of the salt covenant is found in Leviticus 2:13, *"And every oblation of thy meat offering shalt thou season with salt; neither shalt thou suffer the salt of the covenant of thy God to be lacking from thy meat offering: with all thine offerings thou shalt offer salt."* Notice the Lord is giving the children of Israel the strict command to offer salt with every offering. Jesus established this practice in Mark 9:49, when He said, *"And every sacrifice shall be salted with salt."* Here is a tremendous fact concerning the offering of sacrifices. They must be offered with salt. This is the salt of the covenant of thy God, that salt which is offered with a sacrifice. This salt must have savor, or be good salt. In Matthew 5:13, we see Jesus demanding the good salt. He says, *"Ye are the salt of the earth: but if the salt have lost his savour, it is thenceforth good for nothing."* Jesus, referring to good salt, is talking about personal holiness. The Jews to whom He was speaking knew about salt on the sacrifice. They were practicing Jews.

So a part of the salt covenant is to have an offering with good salt on it. Jesus, referring to good salt, is talking about personal holiness, but He is using the Levitical pattern, as He so often did, to explain and illustrate what He is saying and what He desires.

Notice also in Leviticus 2:13, that we have a meat offering. The salt goes on the meat that is offered. A close look at the preceding verses in Leviticus 2 will reveal that this is actually a bread offering. Often the word meat in the Bible is used for substance and not necessarily actual flesh meat. This is the case in verse 13. The "fine flour" that is "baked in cakes" is plainly referring to bread and not meat in Leviticus 2:4, *"And if thou bring an oblation of a meat offering baken in the oven, it shall be unleavened cakes of fine flour mingled with oil or unleavened wafers anointed with oil."* We have bread with salt on it offered unto the Lord. The salt of this offering becomes the salt of the covenant of the Lord. Bread, salt, and sacrifice equal the Salt Covenant.

> ### *It is the salt on the bread offered as a sacrifice that God called a Salt Covenant.*

There is an ancient Middle East custom and tradition that covenants two people together. One party of the intended covenant brings the salt and the other furnishes the bread. They put them together to make an everlasting covenant with each other. Similarly, the Native Americans would enter into a lifelong covenant with one another through blood. Each person would cut himself and put their blood together, making a covenant known to us as blood brothers.

A Messianic Jewish preacher called me from Oregon where he was holding meetings and said, "I had dinner the other night with a group of born again Jordanians. They were telling me about a Middle East custom concerning a covenant between two people. The covenant consisted of one person bringing salt and the other providing bread. One party salted the bread furnished by the other, and they ate it together, creating a covenant." He said, "When I was preaching at the church you pastor, I remember a little tract you had written on the salt covenant. It had on the front a picture of a salt shaker over a loaf of bread with salt falling on the bread. Could you fax this tract to me?" He continued, "Something is going on here. I have been preaching on the bread of Heaven and Jesus being the shewbread. These Jordanians are telling me about the salt. The glory of the Lord is falling in these meetings, but there is something about this salt." I heartily agreed with my friend. There is something about this salt. The Jordanian believers were onto something. This is what the Lord is saying in Leviticus, Chapter 2. Come to me in covenant. Bring an offering of bread and put salt on it and offer it to me.

In Numbers 18:19, we see another reference to the salt covenant. *"All of the heave offerings of the holy things, which the children of Israel offer unto the Lord, have I given thee, and thy sons and thy daughters with thee, by a statute for ever: it is a covenant of salt for ever before the Lord unto thee and to thy seed with thee."* Here we see even stronger language concerning this covenant. Now we see the priesthood to be the partaker of this covenant, and we also see the word *forever,* indicating the perpetuity of the covenant. Additionally, the covenant has been elevated to the seat of *statute.* The priests were offering the heave offerings to the Lord with salt, of course. The Lord received their sacrifice and made a covenant with them. He then declared that they should be given the heave offering, and that it should be a statute forever, or an unchangeable oracle of God. This is a powerful thing. This is also why we will be able to find this covenant so easily in the New Testament under the new covenant. It is a statute for ever, a promise to the priesthood. This promise is to thy sons and daughters. Your sons and daughters will be sustained by the offerings with salt on them. They will actually live on them by consuming them. It is a covenant of salt.

Now we notice by looking at the preceding verses in Numbers 18, that the heave offering talked about in verse 19 is a flesh offering. The bread of Leviticus 2 is now become flesh and is to be consumed by the priesthood after it is offered to the Lord. This is amazing and very important as we look at the contents of the salt covenant. Everything will be in God's divine order: bread, salt, offering, consumed by the priesthood, covenant, statute forever, bread now flesh. It is all there, set in heavenly order or pattern, ready for the new covenant priesthood to grasp. Jesus said He was the bread from Heaven. In John 6:48, He used the words *"that bread."* He said in Matthew 5:13, *"Ye are the salt of the earth."* The salt is part of the sacrifice. We are to be a living salt sacrifice, as we see in Romans 12:1, and that is to be offered unto Him as a priestly offering, holy and acceptable unto Him.

> *Giving to the Lord a personal righteous life as an offering to Him, is the salt of the covenant.*

As priests of the royal priesthood mentioned in I Peter

2:9, we are to consume the bread that is made flesh. It is a spiritual thing, but the Lord Himself gave them bread at the last supper and said concerning that bread, *"This is my flesh,"* or *"This is my body."* When we offer the Lord a personal righteous life as an offering to Him, which is salt, and we partake of the heave offering as priests, we are entering into a very powerful covenant. The Lord declared it a statute forever—a salt covenant. The reality and revelation of this covenant is evident throughout the Bible, as we will see in the following chapters.

Every covenant in the Bible has a certain power and blessing behind it. But all of the covenants are available to mankind through the everlasting covenant of God with man in the pattern the Jew first, then the Gentile. One might notice in the Bible that the term *the covenant* or *the everlasting covenant* is singular. It is because actually there is only one covenant. The term covenants refers to all of the covenants available to us through the one everlasting covenant. The new covenant is in the old. The blood is in the old and the new. The Abrahamic covenant is in the new covenant. The Noahic covenant is a part of the everlasting covenant. All of the covenants of the Bible are in the everlasting covenant.

One of the elders in the church I pastor came to me and said, "The Lord has just revealed to me that I have the blessing of Abraham." He was so blessed with that revelation. It had changed his life. He came to that revelation because he is in the everlasting covenant. That enlightenment could not have come had he not been washed in the blood of the everlasting covenant, which promised that the Lord would bless all of the earth through Abraham. When the Lord revealed that Abrahamic blessing to that elder, it changed his life because he began to embrace the covenant. He had been gloriously saved years ago. I was with him the night he was filled with the Holy Ghost. Even though he was already walking with the Lord the revelation of the Abrahamic covenant brought this powerful new blessing to his life. Why? Because he embraced and believed it by the revelation of the Holy Spirit. Flesh and blood did not reveal that to him. He says, "Every time I talk about it, I get a blessing." What he heard with his spiritual ear, he believed in his spirit. He confessed it with his mouth based on the revelation, and the blessing is his. He will never be the same. So it is with covenant blessings. The everlasting covenant has many covenants in particular. As we see them, embrace them, and believe them, the blessing of that covenant becomes ours.

> ## *In the Salt Covenant the believer must furnish personal righteousness.*

In the salt covenant there is an ingredient that the other covenants do not have, and that is personal righteousness, or salt. What do I bring to the table of the covenant of blood? Just faith, nothing else. But I must bring good salt to put on the bread in the salt covenant. There are two kinds of righteousness. First there is *imputed righteousness*, which cannot be earned and is, of course, the gift of grace. Then there is *personal righteousness*, or salt. That is living a clean and holy life before the Lord. Personal righteousness includes clean hands and a pure heart; it is personal and imputed righteousness. Lot had imputed righteousness, but he didn't have personal righteousness. This is why we call the salt covenant the covenant of responsibility. The believer must bring the salt. The Lord will bring the bread. Embracing this covenant and walking in it contains living clean and holy in this present world, while trusting only the bread. For years now we have noticed that the church in general has been looking for ways to get around this issue of personal holiness and still walk in the power and blessing of the Lord. To walk in this covenant, the believer must understand that one of the ingredients in the contents of this covenant is salt. Again, Jesus said, "*Ye are the salt of the earth.*" The salt covenant is a part of the everlasting covenant just as a true local church is a part of the universal church on earth. The salt covenant is not nearly as well known, but it is just as powerful and needed as any other covenant. As the revelation of His covenants in the covenant starts coming to us, we enter into them by the Lord's divine pattern, and the glory starts falling.

> *What is laid out in the Old Testament should be looked for in the New Testament.*

More and more Christians are beginning to see that God is a covenant God. They are beginning to look into the Old Testament and find the covenants of God. Then they look for their fuller and more spiritual meaning in the New Testament. What the Lord laid out in the Old Testament, He lived out in the New Testament. What is pictured in the Old Testament is produced in the New Testament. A great amount of revelation is coming to the church as a result of the Lord's blessing on the Messianic Jews. Some of the most powerful services on earth are now in the Messianic synagogues. They are seeing Jesus in His glory, and through their help many

Gentile Christians are learning to see Jesus Christ on every page of the Old Testament. They are beginning to see Him in every sacrifice, in every covenant, in every piece of furniture of the tabernacle and the temple. They are embracing the covenants of the everlasting covenant in full revelation, and revival is in the air. Revelation is increasing in Jews and Gentiles alike. There is a stirring in the remnant.

> ### *God will use the Messianic Jews to provoke the Gentile church to restudy the Bible.*

I firmly believe that the Lord used the early Gentile believers to provoke His people Israel to jealousy. I also believe He will now use His people, the Jews, who are full of the revelation of Jesus to provoke the Gentiles to restudy the Word of God, looking for Jesus on every page. A Messianic Jew who preached at the church I pastor made a statement that offended some of the congregation. I understand that He said it out of a heart to see Israel come to Christ, but it did sound a bit strange. He said that the Gentile Christian needs to put his New Testament up and learn who Jesus is in the Old Testament. I immediately thought of Philip in Acts 8:35, *"And began at the same scripture, and preached unto him Jesus."* Of course, all he was using was the Old Testament. Paul was constantly proving that Jesus was Messiah by the Old Testament scriptures. In Acts17:2 and 3, we see him confirming by the scripture Jesus as Messiah by *"opening and alleging"* who He was.

What about the two men on the road to Emmaus after

the crucifixion? They were walking along, despondent and overwhelmed by all that had gone on in Jerusalem. Jesus appeared to them. He talked with them a little then whetted their spiritual appetite. He began to reveal Himself to them. In Luke 24:27 the Bible says, *"And beginning at Moses and all the prophets, He expounded unto them in all the scriptures concerning Himself."* He started in Genesis, the first book of Moses, and showed them who He was. I would love to have heard that glorious discourse. It left them with heavenly heartburn.

We can never win Jews to Jesus without being able to show them from the Old Testament that Jesus is the Christ. Gentile believers are getting acquainted with the Jewishness of the Bible. Messianic Jewish books are selling fast, and in some churches where I go to preach or visit, it is not uncommon to see men and women wearing the telet, or prayer shawl, as they pray. We can not follow Jews back to the ceremonial Levitical law which was never meant for Gentile believers, but we can learn awesome things from their revelation of Jesus in the Old Testament. The salt covenant is a Jewish covenant between the Lord and the Jew first, and we will understand it better when we see its Jewishness. Its contents are all found in the Levitical order of sacrifice and offering. But what the law pictures, Jesus produces.

Jesus, the Bread, is more than the manna typified in the Old Testament.

Jesus is the bread of the salt covenant, not just manna.

WALKING IN THE COVENANT OF SALT

No doubt, the manna typifies Jesus. It was round, which represents no beginning and no end. It was white, which represents purity. It came down from heaven. It had to be picked up after it fell, which represents the necessity of receiving Jesus to become a child of God. There are many other ways the manna typifies Christ. However, many Messianic Jews believe that the deeper revelation of Jesus as bread was the showbread, which by interpretation is the bread that shows His face. He is the bread of the presence of Jehovah. Every sacrifice and every piece of furniture in the temple is very important. To the Jew, the shewbread on that table is the very important testimony of the presence of their Lord. This is one of the many reminders of Emmanuel, or God with us. After the bread had served its time on the table in the inner court of the tabernacle, it was then given to the priests to eat. No one else was supposed to eat it. Jesus referred to this in Luke 6:4, when He spoke of David eating the shewbread when he was running from Saul. The Bible states, *"How he went into the house of God, and did take and eat the shewbread, and gave also to them that were with him; which it is not lawful to eat but for the priests alone."* David was not Levitical, but in his loins was the high priest after the order of Melchisedec, and David's Psalms proves that he knew it. He ate the bread with the revelation of the new order of priesthood coming under the new covenant, the Lord Jesus being our high priest. Under the Levitical order, priests had the priesthood conferred onto them by a ceremonial washing.

Jesus, being our high priest, baptized us by one Spirit into the body of the priesthood. That is why His church is called a royal priesthood. We were washed by the high priest; this also makes us priests. We can eat the bread. Blessed be the

THE CONTENTS OF THE COVENANT OF SALT

Lord! Oh, taste and see that the Lord is good. Jesus said whoever would eat this bread would never hunger again. He said, *"Your fathers did eat manna in the wilderness and are dead."* Manna was God's provision for His people, but the shewbread was the testimony of His presence with them. Only the priests could eat this bread. The bread pictured in the covenant of salt is Jesus, and the salt is the personal righteousness of the believer who has received the bread.

The third time we see the term *salt covenant* is in 2 Chronicles 13:4 and 5, *"And Abijah stood upon mount Zemaraim, which is in mount Ephraim, and said, Hear me, thou Jeroboam, and all Israel; Ought ye not to know that the Lord God of Israel gave the kingdom over Israel to David for ever, even to him and to his sons by a covenant of salt?"* This is very interesting, especially when you see the scenario behind Abijah's powerful statement. There is war between him and Jeroboam, between Israel and Judah, with Jeroboam being the king of Israel and Abijah the king of Judah. Abijah is outnumbered two to one. He has four hundred thousand soldiers. Jeroboam has eight hundred thousand soldiers. Both of their armies are arrayed for battle. They are ready to fight. Abijah stops before they engage in war and says to Jeroboam and all of Israel, "There is something you ought to know before we proceed, and that is that we are walking in the covenant of salt, and you can't overcome us." This is an astounding statement for one so outnumbered. He then proceeds to preach Mr. Jeroboam one of the straightest and most powerful messages in the Word. During the message he lists every single one of the ingredients of the covenant of salt. He systematically shows Jeroboam why he and his army of eight hundred thousand men are not walking in the covenant. Abijah actually lists Jeroboam's sins, pointing them out to him very articulately.

> ## *Abijah is walking*
> ## *in the Covenant of Salt.*

Oh, what a preacher this Abijah is! He is definitely a salt preacher! He wants Jeroboam to understand that his army is going to lose this war because the Lord will not honor him. It is impossible for the Lord to honor him because he is not walking in the salt covenant. Abijah also rehearses in the ears of Jeroboam the contents of the covenant. Now this proves to me that King Jeroboam was familiar with the salt covenant. This is war. He is very careful to speak.

They are about to engage in the largest war in the history of Israel. One million two hundred thousand soldiers are on the ground. Abijah is not going to talk to Jeroboam in terms he can not understand. He is not going to waste time in getting his point across. This is why he mentions the salt covenant first. He knows Jeroboam, being a Jew, will understand the term *salt covenant*. Then Abijah goes into detail as to why his army, Judah, is walking in the covenant and the army of Jeroboam is not.

Abijah says in verse 6, *"Yet Jeroboam the son of Nebat, the servant of Solomon the son of David, is risen up, and is rebelled against his Lord."* Abijah is pointing out to him that he is nothing but a servant to the Davidic dynasty and that he is full of rebellion. In other words, he is a rebellious slave. What a powerful point to make! He was fearless, which is one of the results of walking in the salt covenant.

He is saying, "Jeroboam, you're not a king; you are a rebellious slave. I am a king in the royal order of Rehoboam,

Solomon, and David. You are a rebel." Rebellion is not salt covenant material. They both knew of Samuel's words to Saul in 1 Samuel 15:23, *"Rebellion is as the sin of witchcraft."* It is not one of the ingredients of any of God's covenants. It is certainly not in the salt covenant. Abijah then points out in verse 7, *"And there are gathered unto him vain men, the children of Belial, and have strengthened themselves against Rehoboam the son of Solomon, when Rehoboam was young and tenderhearted, and could not withstand them."* In other words, "You are not separated from the ruthless heathens that have always hated righteousness, but you run with them and hire them, and you are one of them." Abijah is exposing Jeroboam's sin which is certainly not behavior that is conducive to the salt covenant. If you are going to covenant with the Lord, you have to come out from among them and be separated. You can not run with every vile creature and maintain personal holiness. You must be separated.

> ## *Walking in the Salt Covenant gives believers great boldness.*

Abijah then states in verse 8: *"And now ye think to withstand the kingdom of the Lord in the hand of the sons of David; and ye be a great multitude, and there are with you golden calves, which Jeroboam made you for gods."* Abijah is saying, "You are trusting in your big bad army instead of the Lord because your heart is turned to idols, man made little gods, golden calves in particular." I think I hear Abijah saying, "How do you really expect to win a victory against a people who are in the salt covenant with the Lord when you are full of idolatry?" Idolatry is certainly not one of the ingredients of the salt covenant.

In the next verse, Abijah mentions Israel's misdealing with the Levitical priesthood. He says in verse 9, *"Have ye not cast out the priests of the Lord, the sons of Aaron, and the Levites, and have made you priests after the manner of the nations of other lands? So that whosoever cometh to consecrate himself with a young bullock and seven rams, the same may be a priest of them that are no gods."*

Abijah is telling Jeroboam that there is no his army can have any success in this war because they have not only dishonored the holy priesthood, but they have made an unholy priesthood to match their vain, wicked idolatry. This priesthood consists of wicked priests made by wicked men to serve wicked idols. This is certainly not in agreement with the contents of the salt covenant which embraces the true and holy priesthood.

You must admit that this is one of the hottest sermons in the Bible, and it was delivered at one of the most inconvenient moments. It reminds one of Paul when he was almost beaten to death for preaching Jesus to the Jews in Acts, Chapter 21. They wanted to kill him, but when the crowd was silenced, Paul asked for permission to speak then started preaching again, giving testimony of how Jesus saved him. Abijah is that kind of preacher. He is fearless and full of power. May I say he possesses covenant power.

Now, Abijah starts telling Jeroboam what is in the camp of the salt covenant people. He says in verse 10, *"But as for us, the Lord is our God, and we have not forsaken Him; and the priests, which minister unto the Lord, are the sons of Aaron, and the Levites wait upon their business:"* In other words, "Mr. Jeroboam, you will not find any idols over in the salt covenant camp. We haven't forsaken God like you have. We are in a covenant with our God. He is our God, and He is not competing with any other god for our devotion." Notice that Abijah is also pointing out to Jeroboam that in his camp are the genuine bonafide priests of the living God, after the order of Levi and Aaron, his seed. We will see the significance of this more fully in the chapter entitled "The Priesthood and the Salt Covenant."

Abijah is mentioning three levels of priesthood here in order to make his point to Jeroboam: the priests, the Levites, and the sons of Aaron. All Levites were not sons of Aaron. All Levites were not active priests at all times, because they served the priesthood in order of their courses, which was a period of time they were to serve in rotation. But all of the sons of Aaron were sons of the Levitical order, which is the priestly tribe of Israel. Abijah no doubt includes this comment about Aaron because Aaron is the first high priest. All of the order of the priesthood was subject to his conferment according to the Law of Moses. Aaron and his sons are the only people who can confer the Levites into the holy priesthood. Abijah is saying this to reprove Jeroboam for the way he acquired his priests. In other words, Abijah is saying, "We have the right priesthood, and we attained them the right way. The priests who are active in their course of service are with us. The ones who are not active are with us, and it is all in order through the Aaronic order." Sounds like a royal priesthood to me. Sounds like a kingdom of priests to me. Now this is salt covenant material.

The sacrifice and the incense is with the Salt Covenant people.

Abijah goes on to say concerning the priests in verse 11, *"And they burn unto the Lord every morning and every evening burnt sacrifices and sweet incense: the shewbread also set they in order upon the pure table: and the candlestick of gold with the lamps thereof, to burn every evening: for we keep the charge of the Lord our God: but ye have forsaken Him."* All of this is salt covenant contents. We know that the sacrifice and the incense is translated in the new covenant to praise and prayer. We already know the shewbread typifies Jesus, setting on the pure table.

See the contents of the covenant here: We keep the charge, Abijah is saying, and we have the bread of His presence, the bread and the salt. He is saying, "Look, Jeroboam, you can not defeat us because we are walking in a powerful covenant with our Lord. We are walking in personal righteousness. We are a praying people. We are a praising people. We have the bread."

Abijah goes on to tell him in the next verse that the captain for their army is God Himself, and then he pleads with Jeroboam not to fight against them because he cannot win. I believe that Abijah knows the outcome of this battle. He has a great confidence in this covenant. He is not in the least concerned about losing the war. He doesn't want Jeroboam to fight against them, not because he is scared, but because he hates to see what is about to happen to so many Jews. Abijah understands the covenant. He knows the contents are all there. Great poise and courage is all over him. He is anointed from head to toe. He is able to preach a plain, pointed and powerful sermon right in the face of his adversary. In spite of his powerful delivery, Jeroboam refuses to listen to this sermon, and goes right into the war against his fellow Jews, only to cause the largest slaughter of men in one day ever to be recorded in history—right up to this very day in which we live. Five hundred thousand men died in one day. The covenant people prevailed. Abijah was right. The contents of the covenant were all there: the bread, the salt that had savor, the sacrifice, and the correct priesthood, all in divine order. The glorious victory here of the salt covenant people should be a timeless reminder to the church. Covenant people prevail over their enemies because they please their God.

CHAPTER TWO

THE BALANCE OF THE COVENANT

One of the most magnificent qualities that walking in the covenant of salt produces is a tremendous balance. This is certainly one of the most severely needed attributes in the body of Christ today is balance. For years, we have watched the destruction in the body caused by a lack of scriptural balance. Honest well-meaning Christians are majoring on minors and minoring on majors, going past the Bible emphasis on any given subject or theme, then building a movement behind it or upon it.

We have seen almost fad-like waves of manifestations in just the past few years that are caused by this lack of balance. These waves could never have gained credibility among sincere Christians if they were not at least somewhat supported by the Bible. However, the over emphasis, or should we say lack of balance, on the given subject or theme has caused a great many shipwrecks in the faith. Even stout-hearted Christians have ridden these waves, only later to see that they were actually produced by a lack of Bible balance. The prosperity movement, the faith movement, the glossila or tongues movement, the falling in the spirit movement, and the laughing movement are a few in the recent list of waves of manifestations overly emphasized. Again, it isn't that these things mentioned are not biblical, but it is the lack of balance that brings the destruction. It is not wise to attack any Biblical manifestation. However, we must certainly push for the balance that the Bible places on them.

God does want us to prosper and be in good health, as our soul prospers. But if our emphasis on prosperity goes beyond the emphasis put on the subject by the Bible, then it no longer a blessing, thus becoming a snare. Of course, God does want us to have faith. Without faith we cannot please God, but faith without works is dead.

God does want us to speak with tongues. Paul said, *"I would that ye all spake with tongues,"* but Paul did not make that the criteria for fellowship or fullness. The three on Mount Transfiguration did fall in the awesome presence of the Lord. But many have developed this into an art, with catchers and coverings. Laughter does do good like a medicine. To go to church with the intention of laughing or getting people to laugh is a terrible over emphasis on the matter. It is the over emphasis of any of these manifestations that has caused so much confusion. Then, when some balanced believer, out of grief for the cause of Christ, calls the body back to the Bible balance, he is labeled as negative and judgmental. The problem is lack of balance.

> ## *The Salt Covenant insures the believer a safe Bible balance.*

The salt covenant is the only Bible covenant that keeps the

believer safe from a lack of balance. Honest Christ-seeking believers will confess that they have a problem with balance. Most will readily admit this and are crying out for help in the matter. For instance, the balance between grace and truth can be a problem for Christians to maintain. The Bible says in John 1:14 that Jesus was *"full of grace and truth."* What a tremendous testimony concerning the Master! Most of us are either short on grace or short on the truth. It is a struggle to maintain that particular balance. We emphasize the grace, and we get so sweet that we go to the point of compromise. We are ready to join the ecumenical movement. We don't want to make any waves or make anyone uncomfortable. We just want to fit in and be sweet. Then we come to our senses and say to ourselves, "I'm just too sweet, and I'm going to stand on the Word of God, and I don't care who likes it or who doesn't." Then we go on the warpath for truth, ready to march on Washington or protest something or someone. We are ready to rip up anyone who seems a little wishy-washy. We take a good position, but we develop a bad disposition. Then we wake up and decide that we have been so mean and lacking in compassion with everyone that we need to be a little sweeter. We start the whole process over again. Grace and truth, what a balance! Jesus, walking in that balance, knew just when to blast a hypocrite and when to pick up a repentant sinner.

> ### *The Master is the master of balance.*

Compassion and conviction were mixed perfectly in the Master. It is evident that the body of Christ has great trouble in this area. When the compassion rules we become liberals, and when the conviction rules, we become legalists. It is hard to discern which one is the most damaging to the body.

What about zeal and knowledge? Now that is another hard balance to keep. We have seen a lot of imbalance in this area. It is dangerous to be around people with great zeal and little knowledge. People with knowledge and no zeal are a thorn in a church's side. The theologian said to the evangelist, "I have seen very few of your kind with great knowledge." The evangelist said to the theologian, "I have yet to see one of your kind with any fire."

In a little town not far from the church I pastor, a dear fellow preacher conducted services regularly in a nursing home. He was a solid brother and wanting always to help young preachers get established in the ministry. A young preacher kept coming to the nursing home attending meetings, wanting to preach. After a lot of persuasion and pleading, my dear preacher friend finally set him up to preach the next service.

The meeting was held in the lobby of the facility. The nurses would roll the residents up to the lobby in wheelchairs helping them up to the meetings by walking beside them. Some were on crutches; some used walkers, but with great effort they would come to the meetings. The time came for the young, zealous preacher to preach to the residents.

My friend didn't know that the young preacher had just been listening to a taped message of a hot sermon on one to one soul winning and street evangelism. The young man wasn't preaching long until he was screaming at the residents about their need to be out on the streets, knocking on doors. He was out of it, just preaching to them with a tremendous zeal. He said, "You lay around this rest home and your friends and neighbors are going to Hell. Every one of you should be out there winning souls."

He went on to upbraid them for not having visitors sitting beside them. He scolded them for their evangelical laziness. My preacher friend sat there astonished and was about to pull on the young preacher's reins when a little 90 year old lady pulled his coat sleeve and said, "Brother, does he know where he is?" My preacher friend said, "Ma'am, I am afraid he doesn't."

This is a classic example of zeal without knowledge. What about the folks who know exactly how things ought to be done? They have the knowledge but don't have the zeal to do it. These folks are the critics in the ministry. How we need the balance of zeal and knowledge!

> ### *A lack of balance always brings confusion.*

Another difficult balance is faith and works. One fellow says, "I'm just going to believe the Lord and do nothing but thank God for the results I want." He can quote a lot of verses on why he is right and how it is all going to happen, but he winds up disenchanted, and another shipwreck occurs because of a lack of balance. The other man says, "I will work and get it done. You faith people are off, and I'm just going to make it happen by good old fashioned hard work." He goes into some crazy phase of Christian humanism and winds up in a mess. This is a difficult balance for the believer. James had to deal with that lack of balance. He said in James 2:15-17, *"If a brother or sister be naked, and destitute of daily food, and one of you say unto them, depart in peace, be ye warmed and filled; notwithstanding ye give them not those things which are needful to the body; what doth it profit? Even so faith, if it hath not works, is dead, being alone."* He continues to stress the need for balance by saying in verse 18, *"Yea, a man may say, thou hast faith, and I have works; shew me thy faith without thy works, and I will shew thee my faith by my works."* James saw the need for balance between faith and works in his day. We can all see it today.

> ### *An unbalance makes the believer often unable to hear Bible truths.*

I was preaching in Albuquerque a few years ago and had the opportunity to attend the ministry of a preacher who called himself a faith teacher. In his message, he continued to pick on the Apostle Paul, putting him down because he suffered a lot and went through a lot of trials. I confronted the minister about it afterwards, and the response I got was shocking. I was told in no uncertain words that Paul was weak in his faith walk and that he had no business confessing defeat all of the time. I was told that if Paul had stood on the Word like he should have, he would have rebuked the persecution he went through and would never have felt any pain. I was told that Jesus is the example for the believer, not Paul. I told the preacher that it was Jesus who told Paul that he would suffer many things for Him (Acts 9:16) and that Jesus suffered even more than Paul (Luke 9:22). He couldn't even hear my words, even though I gave him scripture and verse. He had gotten so out of balance in one area that he couldn't hear the plain simple truth of the Word.

I am thoroughly convinced that walking in the covenant of salt will bring the balance in all these areas that is so badly needed. Really, it is the lack of balance in the church of Corinth that Paul is constantly addressing. They were emphasizing the gifts and the power more than love. This is another hard balance, power and love. 1 Corinthians 13 brings us back to the balance of love and power. There is a cry in the body of Christ today for the good scriptural balanced teaching and preaching.

> ### *We need to have the great toe of our spiritual right foot anointed.*

In the Old Testament, when the priests were conferred into the priesthood and consecrated to the ministry, they had to go through quite a ritual, and it included several different anointings and applications of blood. We read about some of these procedures in Exodus 29:20, *"Then shalt thou kill the ram, and take his blood, and put it upon the tip of the right ear of Aaron, and upon the tip of the right ear of his sons, and upon the thumb of their right hand, and upon the great toe of their right foot, and sprinkle the blood upon the altar round about."* The ear had to hear right for the priesthood to be effective. The hand had to grip right in order for the priest to hold on to the things of God. But the big toe is necessary for the walk of balance. This is so important for those who are now walking in the new covenant priesthood. *"He that hath an ear let him hear."* Let us hold fast to that which is right and good, and let our big toe be anointed with the blood that we may walk in a holy balance before the Lord.

In the salt covenant, we have the bread and the salt as the main ingredients. Jesus said, *"I am the bread"* in John 6:48, and He said, *"Ye are the salt"* in Matthew 5:13. Bread is grace, and salt is works or personal righteousness. Grace or imputed righteousness and salt—it is hard to find this balance in the body. I have visited some bread churches with little salt, and I have visited some salt churches with little bread. I have seen some salty Christians with little bread, and I have seen some bread Christians with little salt. But I haven't seen too many that have the bread with salt on the sacrifice. Salt is a seasoning and it produces a certain flavor. If that flavor is not there, it is amazingly noticeable. So it is in a church that has no salt in it. There is no real conviction of sin.

The pastors of these churches give fruitless altar calls which are nothing more than a pitiful exhibit of powerless preaching full of the persuasion of men and horribly lacking the anointing of the Holy Ghost. Why? There is no salt. In the bread only churches, and there are plenty of them, the people never change their community because they are full of compromise, secret sins, and worldly desires. It is no small wonder that they have no influence on a lost community. They are like Lot in Sodom. Everybody blames the perverts in Sodom and Gomorrah for the destruction of those cities, and certainly perversion is a wicked sin before the Lord. But it was not the homosexual community that caused the mass destruction of this metropolitan area. The truth is it was caused by the pitiful bread only church that Brother Lot had going. He had no salt in his life. In 2 Peter 2:7 we find this testimony concerning Lot: *"And delivered just Lot, vexed with the filthy conversation of the wicked."* Because he had no salt, Lot compromised and sat in the gate of the city, allowing his righteous soul to be vexed by seeing and hearing the wicked population.

> ### *There can be no good salt without separation.*

Where there is no separation from the world, there is no salt for the bread. Lot had the bread, because the Bible says *"just Lot."* This phrase does not mean *only* Lot. It means *justified* Lot. The Greek word here is *dikaios*, meaning justified, or made righteous. That is grace, and that is the bread. It is a perfect example of a bread only church. Its members are sitting in front of heathens all of the time, through audio and video entertainment, which by the way is America's number one passion. They are vexing their righteous souls and can not understand why they have no influence over their own families, much less their neighbors.

When the Lord sent two angels to deliver justified Lot from the coming destruction, his own family members didn't take him seriously. Genesis 19:14 says, *"And Lot went out, and spake unto his sons in law, which married his daughters, and said, Up, get you out of this place; for the Lord will destroy this city, but he seemed as one that mocked unto his sons in law."* There was no salt in his life. Lot's Uncle Abraham had already interceded before the Lord for that city, and the Lord agreed to spare the city if there were ten righteous souls there. But there were not. What a pitiful testimony for a justified person living in a metropolitan area not to have at least ten converts, and that includes his immediate family. His own wife had Sodom in her soul. The haunting words of the poem of Isaac Watts comes ringing to the ears of the bread only churches in America, "Lot in Sodom no gain, no gain, saint in darkness what shame, what shame."

THE BALANCE OF THE COVENANT

Lot had no salt for Sodom.

The lack of salt is such a problem in our American churches. It is no wonder that the Lord turned Lot's wife into the pillar of salt. Now you know why He used salt. He could have turned her into anything He wanted. The Lord turned Lot's wife into what she had refused to be. He turned her into what could have saved the entire metropolitan area, salt.

She disobeyed and looked back into the doomed cities because her heart was there. Anybody whose heart is in the world can not have the salt with savor. The scripture says in 1 John 2:15, *"Love not the world, neither the things that are in the world. If any man love the world, the love of the Father is not in him."*

If Lot had been walking in the covenant of salt, the city would not have been destroyed. One can readily see the devastation and doom caused by this lack of balance, bread but no salt.

I had the privilege of sitting in the home of Brother Leonard Ravenhill, who was so gracious to invest some of his time in a young undernourished preacher. Toward the close of our conversation, I asked him, "What is the reason for the powerless church we see on earth today?" This broken hearted intercessor for the nation looked at me with those eyes of fire and said, "It is the *if* and the *when*." He could tell by my expression that I didn't have a clue what he meant. Needless to say, he had my full attention. I had driven from Kentucky all the way to Texas with no other business but to sit at his feet for an hour or so. (May I say it was a worthwhile trip.)

> ## *The church, in general, has a light attitude toward sin.*

He proceeded to show me the prevailing attitude in the churches of America today. He quoted 1 John 2:1, *"My little children, these things write I unto you, that ye sin not. And if any man sin, we have an advocate with the Father, Jesus Christ the righteous."* He said, "The attitude of the church is *when* we sin and not *if* we sin. People think they have to sin every day and that they can't help it. Most Christians don't even expect to go a whole day without sinning." He went on to upbraid what I call bread only churches for their lack of personal holiness, which is salt. No wonder the church is so anemic. The word coming forth from the bread only pulpits is not even close to *"Holy men of God moved by the Holy Ghost."* The Bible says in Colossians 4:6 to *"Let your speech be always with grace, seasoned with salt, that ye may know how ye ought to answer every man."* Saltless ministries of saltless ministers have no influence, and henceforth no fruitfulness. Brother Ravenhill said it is the plague of the Western church.

In the ministry of Elisha we see that he ran onto a problem like this in the city of ancient Jericho. In 2 Kings 2:19, we find these words, *"And the men of the city said unto Elisha, behold I pray thee, the situation of this city is pleasant, as my Lord seeth: but the water is naught, and the ground barren."* Everything looked good, but the water was bad so the ground was barren. They were saying, "There is something horribly lacking in this place, and we can't produce anything unless it gets fixed." This is the exact situation of the saltless churches

29

or bread only churches all over the land. Everything looks good as they go through the motions and continue with a form of Godliness, but nothing is bearing real fruit. The salt covenant can fix it. With every sacrifice, there must be salt. What does Brother Elisha do? He knew exactly what to do. Verse 20 says, *"And he said, bring me a new cruse, and put salt therein. And they brought it to him."* In verse 21, the Bible says, *"And he went forth unto the spring of the waters, and cast the salt in there, and said, Thus saith the Lord, I have healed these waters; there shall not be from thence any more death or barren land."* It took the salt to make it work.

> ## *There has to be salt on the bread before true revival comes.*

The air in this nation is getting thick with expectancy of revival. Many are seeking the Lord for a powerful move that will literally change the moral climate of our land. This is wonderful and exciting, but if there is no salt in the believer's sacrifice, it will not work. Every true move of God fully embraced personal holiness, or salt. There must be a balance, and that balance is produced in the believer by the salt covenant. A lack of balance is always devastating to the body. The devil is fairly well pleased if we stop short of the truth. He is also pleased if we go past it. His goal is to see that we don't rest right on it. Rightly dividing the word of truth is resting right on it, in a holy attitude with scriptural balance. This is a rarity.

Just as harmful to the body as the bread only crowd is the salt only ecclesia. When personal righteousness is exalted to such a degree as to make it a means of attaining God, death begins to rule. Salt only churches are usually trying to work their way into Heaven, and trying to find favor with the Lord by their deeds of righteousness. The Pharisaical spirit begins to rise, and there is not a precious soul around that can escape the pitiful condemnation and criticism of this death.

> ## *There is death in "salt only" ministry.*

The Apostle Paul was constantly fighting this spirit in his day. He told young Timothy in 2 Timothy 2:1, *"Thou therefore, my son, be strong in the grace that is in Christ Jesus."* Stay with the bread, Timothy. The salt is not the sacrifice; it goes on the sacrifice.

If there is salt and no bread, there is death. It is easy to see the struggle of the balance of bread and salt. All through the New Testament, Paul would give them bread or grace, and teach them to live holy, which is the covenant. The Judiazers would come right behind him and try to put the people back into bondage by over emphasizing the salt, or in their case, the keeping of the ceremonial Law of Moses, as a way or means of salvation.

Paul was so disturbed by this salt only doctrine concerning the churches in Galatia that his letter abandons his usual format of plus minus plus, for which the Pauline epistles are noted. In this sandwich approach to edification, Paul would start his letters with a very profound commendation to the church to which he was writing. In the middle, he would give the reproof and rebuke, then end with some wonderful words of motivation and encouragement.

The Balance of the Covenant

This is not true with the book of Galatians. He gets right to the problem in Chapter one, and as early as verse 6, he says, *"I marvel that ye are so soon removed from Him that called you into the grace of Christ unto another gospel."* Why such rebuke so early in the epistle? Paul could smell the death that always comes when there is no bread. He goes on to tell them that they have been bewitched by gospel perverts. He addresses this same crowd in Romans 10:3, *"For they being ignorant of God's righteousness, (bread) and going about to establish their own righteousness, (salt) have not submitted themselves unto the righteousness of God."*

Modern day Judaizers destroy through "salt only" doctrine.

The devil was working through the Judiazers of that day to destroy the balance of the early church and bring those liberated saints back under the bondage of the law, which is death. Paul says in Galatians 5:1, *"Stand fast therefore in the liberty wherewith Christ hath set us free, and be not entangled again with the yoke of bondage."* He even tells them if they are trusting in the works of the law (which refers to the ceremonial Law of Moses), that they are falling from grace, or leaving grace behind. Paul knew the horrible demise of trusting in his own good works. Man has a religious tendency anyway, and the death doctrine of working for grace has always beleaguered the body of Christ.

John Wesley, the tremendous, tireless itinerant evangelist of the 1700s was accused by his peers of preaching works or personal righteousness as the means of salvation, even though he plainly walked in the balance of the salt covenant.

He said to his critics in a letter when he was in his sixties, "I ascribe the whole of salvation to the mere grace of God and find it to be the privilege and duty of all recipients of that wonderful grace to live absolutely clean and holy in this life." This is the right balance, and it is the salt on the bread or the salt covenant.

Paul, in the book of Titus, is saying exactly the same thing. He says in Chapter 3, beginning at verse 5, *"Not by works of righteousness which we have done, but according to His mercy, he saved us, by the washing of regeneration, and renewing of the Holy Ghost; which He shed on us abundantly through Jesus Christ our Savior; that being justified by His grace, we should be made heirs according to the hope of eternal life. This is a faithful saying, and these things I will that thou affirm constantly, that they which have believed in God might be careful to maintain good works. These things are good and profitable unto men."* If men vacillate on the great Bible doctrine of justification by faith, then all of their works and effort have the stench of death on them. Paul said in Galatians 2:16, *"Knowing that a man is not justified by the works of the law, but by the faith of Jesus Christ, even we have believed in Jesus Christ, that we might be justified by the faith of Christ, and not by the works of the law: for by the works of the law shall no flesh be justified."*

> ## *John Wesley was a Salt Covenant preacher.*

John Wesley preached holiness of thought and deed as a way of life. He and his Methodist preachers stood for entire sanctification of the believer, but never once did he trust in that for the atonement for sin. He simply salted down the bread with his personal holiness. All he did was change the history of the nation of England. Even secular history stated that the Wesleyan revivals in England spared the nation from the French Revolution. When the balance is right, the glory falls.

You must have the salt to be effective, but if you exalt it out of its place, it will cause great spiritual cancer and spread its claws of death everywhere. Elisha the prophet again shows us through another one of his miracles the importance of having the bread. We find this account in 2 Kings 4:38-41, *"And Elisha came again to Gilgal; and there was a dearth in the land; and the sons of the prophets were sitting before him: and he said unto his servant, Set on the great pot, and seethe pottage for the sons of the prophets. And one went out into the field to gather herbs, and found a wild vine, and gathered thereof wild gourds his lap full, and came and shred them into the pot of pottage: for they knew them not. So they poured out for the men to eat. And it came to pass, as they were eating of the pottage, that they cried out, and said, O thou man of God, there is death in the pot. And they could not eat thereof. But he said, Then bring meal. And he cast it into the pot; and he said, Pour out for the people, that they may eat. And there was no harm in the pot."* Isn't it amazing that it took meal *bread* to heal the death in the pot? One of those young prophets gathered a lap full of wild gourds and shredded them up and put them in the soup. It would have killed them all if Elisha hadn't known what to do. He got some meal and healed it. Again, if it doesn't have bread in it, there is death in the pot.

How many precious souls even now are eating death every week from the churches they attend? They eat the death of struggling to get to heaven in their own power, the death of critical condemnation spewing from a self-righteous fountain, the stench of wild vines and gourds which were never meant to be consumed by the sons of the prophets. They have no life, no joy, no vitality, just death and fear. Legalism is death in the pot. Oh, man of God, get the bread! Get some meal and throw it in the pot before we die! In Jericho, Elisha put salt in the water to bring the productivity to the land. In Gilgal, he put bread in the pot to get rid of the death. It seems to me that Elisha knew something of the salt covenant.

My wife and I were in Wilmore, Kentucky at the campus of Asbury College. Our daughter was enrolling there, and we wanted to go and check it out. I was anxious to visit the Hughes Auditorium, where the great revival began in February, 1970. When we went into that building, we began to sense the power of the Holy Spirit. No one said anything or did anything to cause it, but we both began to cry. I looked at my wife and she looked at me. Each of us was saying to the other with our expression, "You feel it, too." We were aware that this was a special place to the Lord and that wonderful things had happened here. I had been preaching and studying the salt covenant for some time and had learned when there is that kind of anointing, I could find some sign of the covenant. It was not just a blessing, but more of an awareness of a holy God and a spiritual habitation. I remember thinking of what I had read about that great outpouring in that building. The first service alone lasted over a hundred and eighty hours, with true repentance and a hovering of the presence of Jesus that brought everyone on the campus into the move.

THE BALANCE OF THE COVENANT

> ## *The great revival at Asbury was in the Salt Covenant balance.*

I had read how people stood in line for hours to confess their sins to the assembly and commit their ways unto the Lord. The whole area was affected. I knew that this move of God was encompassed by repentance and personal holiness. I knew the salt covenant had to have something to do with it. I was pondering on the thought and scarcely listening to our guide.

Upon leaving the sanctuary, we paused on the front steps for a moment, and I looked up on the building to a marble plaque embedded in the brickwork. As I read it, I said, "That's it. There is the great salt covenant that no doubt the founders of Asbury College walked in and preached." The plaque read: "Free salvation for all men—full salvation from all sin." Free salvation, that's the grace. That is the bread. Full salvation from all sin. That is the salt of holiness. Again, when the balance is right, the glory falls.

My heart breaks for the body to enter into the balance the salt covenant affords. The stench of death would be gone, and the wonderful water of productivity would flow into beautiful life and vitality, literally producing a thirst for God in everyone who witnesses it. An unquenchable hunger for the things of God will absolutely come upon those around this kind of balance, and it is only produced through walking in the salt covenant.

CHAPTER THREE

THE CONTENTMENT IN THE COVENANT

Walking in the covenant of salt produces a glorious peace and constant joy for the believer. In a time when the clamor of the world is so loud, there is still a place for the child of God to walk where he can experience the bliss of heaven on earth. I firmly believe that it is time for the new covenant priesthood to challenge the Christian world to begin to walk in this type of open heaven that the scripture affords. Away with the legalistic condemnation that chokes the life out of the church! On the other hand, away with the light, entertaining, soft on sin, crossless, compromising, and fruitless message of modern Pentecost. Now is the time for the true remnant to begin to walk in genuine holiness and the glorious contentment the abundant life produces. Life which can be described as heaven on earth is what the covenant of salt yields.

> *The glory of heaven on earth*
> *is available through the Salt Covenant.*

THE CONTENTMENT IN THE COVENANT

I had just finished a radio message on the elevated level of a life walking in the Spirit brings when I received a call from a minister in the area. This was his complaint, "Brother Miller, you are far too lofty in your preaching of such matters, for who can live on such a plane?" He was not mean-spirited at all. He was shaken to the bottom of his soul by the Holy Ghost. He was overwhelmed by the very thought of the possibility of actually living in the victory walk of holiness while trusting only in the shed blood of Jesus for salvation. He was really saying, "Preacher, tell me it is true. Tell me you're right." He went on to tell me that he had been living in total frustration, and that he was actually under the persuasion that he would have to live in defeat for the rest of his life, with the flesh popping up to rule again every time it so desired. I had the privilege of showing him in the Bible the wonderful delight of walking in the flesh but not warring

> *Walking after the Spirit brings the believer great contentment.*

after the flesh. Everybody leaves Paul in the book of Romans, chapter 7, wanting to do what is right but not being able to do so. He said in verse 19, *"For the good that I would I do not: but the evil which I would not, that I do."* How many Christians have camped out on this verse and said in their heart, "See, I am just like Paul." The truth is Paul did not live there at all, and neither should the new covenant priesthood of believers. Paul was explaining the death of living there. He was preparing us to walk in the next chapter where he talks of walking without condemnation because he is after the Spirit and not the flesh. Paul definitely walked in the salt covenant. He walked in the victory of the Lord. There really is a victory march this side of heaven.

There is great contentment for the child of God, who is walking after the Spirit, and not the flesh, free from the law of death and sin. This is only produced by the operation of grace, or the bread. Paul described this walk of holy contentment in 2 Corinthians 10:3, *"For though we walk in the flesh, we do not war after the flesh."* That doesn't sound like defeat to me. It doesn't have the sound of turmoil of heart and frustration of soul that I see everywhere in the body of Christ. Paul goes on to say in verse 4, *"For the weapons of our warfare are not carnal, but mighty through God to the pulling down of strong holds."* This is the abundant life. In verse 5, we see the open heaven: *"Casting down imaginations, and every high thing that exalteth itself against the knowledge of God, and bringing into captivity every thought unto the obedience of Christ."* Too lofty? If it is, then it's time we were just absolutely too lofty.

It was old Dr. Denman, the austere but respected Methodist preacher of a generation ago, who offended some of his minister friends with his bold and intriguing answer to the question, "What will heaven be like?" His simply reply, "Just like it is here." brought both astonished looks and perplexed groans from his contemporaries. Dr. Denman was not referring to the lack of pain and tears in heaven which will certainly distinguish that grand place from this world. He was referring to the absolute Lordship of Christ over his life, and the open heaven that he walked under in this life. He wasn't boasting. He was provoking them to go on to the holy hill of the Lord.

It perturbs me that the ministers of this generation have not properly challenged the saints of this generation to go on in Jesus. We dance around the outside of the veil too much. We need to be stirred and provoked to move toward the mark of true holiness of thought, word and deed, and rest squarely on the grace of God for redemption. The salt covenant is just that.

> ## *There is joy in the heart that is uncondemned before the Lord.*

Oh the joy of a holy heart resting in his redeemer! What confidence the believer has when his heart does not condemn him! The Bible makes that clear in 1 John 3:21, *"Beloved, if our heart condemn us not, then have we confidence toward God."* Your heart will not condemn you when you are walking in the salt covenant. When we walk in the Spirit, we will not fulfill the lusts of the flesh. Then there is no condemnation.

How many times have I heard only half of Romans 8:1 quoted? *"There is therefore now no condemnation to them which are in Christ Jesus."* We must not stop there, because the salt is left out. Here comes the salt, *"Who walk not after the flesh, but after the Spirit."* How can believers expect to walk before the Lord without condemnation and live carnal fleshly lives? They can't. Real contentment comes from the salt on the bread. There is no question that every time man enters into a covenant with the Lord, that as he walks in that covenant he reaps great benefits. Who can describe the immense satisfaction that comes to the heart of the believer when he has the wonderful assurance that he and his God are at peace, and he is doing that which is pleasing to the Lord? Righteousness is the way into the heart of the Lord Jesus. When we fully trust the matchless grace of Jesus and walk in the Spirit to please Him, it does just that.

The Bible says in Psalm 11:7, *"For the righteous Lord loveth righteousness; His countenance doth behold the upright."* The church in America needs a deep revelation of this wonderful truth. Notice that the Lord's righteousness is mentioned first. This is because there is no other real righteousness except what stems from Him and is produced by Him. The imputed righteousness that the believer has received by grace also enables him to walk in personal righteousness, which is what the Lord really loves. He is always found in that kind of setting. He loves it. I firmly believe that this verse is referring to the joy the Lord receives when we walk in the covenant. The secret of the Lord is there. It is great joy to be under the shadow of the Almighty. It is absolutely no coincidence that the only man in the Bible who was promised an open heaven is also the only man to whom Jesus affirmed that in him was no guile. This is Nathaniel of John, Chapter 1.

> ## *The Lord desires us to covenant with Him.*

In Psalm 25:14 the Bible says, *"The secret of the Lord is with them that fear Him: and He will show them His covenant."* We must covenant with God, for therein is great contentment. Notice in Psalm 91 the wonderful promises for the individual who lives under the shadow of the Almighty. In verse 3 the Word says, *"Surely He shall deliver thee from the snare of the fowler..."* Deliver whom? That one who dwells in the secret place of the Most High. Who dwells there? Worldlings? Seekers of the flesh? God forbid. Dare anyone think for a moment that he will enter into holy, sweet intimacy with the Creator and not walk in personal holiness? Even babes in Christ know better.

I was preaching once on the subject, "The Joy of Holy Living." After the meeting, a middle-aged man walked up to me and said, "You know I had a sneaking suspicion that my worldliness was the reason for my unhappiness in the Lord." I could scarcely believe what I was hearing. Here is a man who, I found out later, had been in the church for years and years but never experienced the abundant life of the salt covenant. He was actually hoping that he could bypass the salt and offer a sacrifice. The Word plainly says in Mark 9:49, *"and every sacrifice shall be salted with salt."* He had never heard true holiness preached. He only knew he was terribly void in his relationship with the Lord. This is so simple but so profound. People who are walking in the absolute victory and joy of the Lord are living clean and holy. There really is profundity in simplicity. Knowing that there is not a thing between you and your redeemer is heaven on earth.

The second part of Psalm 91:3 gives tremendous joy and peace to the salt covenant people. It says, *"And from the noisome pestilence."* He will deliver from noisome pestilence. Strong's concordance translates this noisome pestilence as clamor, horrible clamor. What a promise to those under the shadow of the Almighty! The world's clamor will not affect you. I have found this to be so wonderful. I have peace, peace, wonderful peace. This produces poise, the kind that will draw men and women to Jesus. The clamor is all around you, but not on you. The waves are crashing and the wind is blowing, but you are under His wings. This is the testimony this crazy world needs to see and hear, that we are free from the noisome pestilence because we have ascended to the holy hill with a clean heart and pure hands.

Those Moravians of the 1700's, on the ship with John Wesley, preached a very loud sermon to the disenchanted young evangelist. They preached it with their silence and poise. While the storm raged, the storm that many on the boat thought would mean certain death to all, those Moravians sat quietly in the hull of the ship with perfect poise. Wesley was so taken by it that he asked one of them, "Aren't you fearful at all?" His answer to Wesley, "I thank my God, no." He was under the wings. He was on the holy hill. He was in the secret place.

> ### *The Lord blesses the one*
> ### *He delights in.*

The Lord delights in that washed in the blood saint who brings salt to the sacrifice. Because He delights in him, that saint enjoys a high level of intimacy that lifts him above the clamor of this world and allows him to actually live in an open heaven. It sounds too good to be true, but hear this promise out in Psalm 91:4, *"He shall cover thee with His feathers, under His wings shalt thou trust: His truth shall be thy shield and buckler."* The promise gains power in verses 5 and 6, *"Thou shalt not be afraid for the terror by night; nor for the arrow that flieth by day; nor for the pestilence that walketh in darkness; nor for the destruction that wasteth at noonday."* Actually the entire chapter keeps gaining power of promise until in verse 14, the Word changes tense. Notice the change, *"Because he hath set his love upon Me, therefore will I deliver him: I will set him on high, because he hath known my name."* The psalmist is no longer talking for the

Lord at this point. He was explaining what the Lord will do for those who will walk with Him. Now the Lord is speaking through the psalmist and saying I will reward that individual who sets his love upon Me. Can we really say that we are in love with Jesus and not obey Him? Can we obey Him and not walk in holiness before Him? Can we walk in holiness before the Lord and not have salt?

Jesus said in John 14:15, *"If ye love me, keep my commandments."* He doesn't want lip service. That is not setting your love upon Him. The Lord said he would lift that saint up on high who sets his love upon Him. That is it. That is the holy hill. That is the shadow of His wings. That is the spot between the cherubim where the blue flame of the glory of the Lord dwells. That is contentment with a million exclamation marks! It is joy with a victory shout! Instead of answering the call of the Lord to that lofty place, many will wrestle around at the bottom of the hill, trying to bring the call down instead of going up to the call. How many sick ministries have built a theological death tank for their people simply because they interpreted the verses to fit their lifestyle instead of raising their lifestyle to fit the verses?

Evangelist Rueben Robinson, known as Uncle Buddy, the Nazarene preacher of the early 1900's, was a real champion of the faith who walked in the salt covenant with the Lord. His Baptist preacher friend said to him, "You're the happiest legalist I ever met." Another minister said to him one day, "I would give the world to have the joy and victory that you have." Uncle Buddy's answer was, "That's all it will cost you, my friend."

> *This remnant church*
> *walking in the Salt Covenant*
> *will provoke the body of Christ.*

My wife and I were in Chattanooga at a Sword of the Lord conference where we heard Dr. Curtis Hutson preach. The now deceased editor of the *Sword of the Lord* was preaching on separation from the world. He quoted a portion of Uncle Buddy's message about the second blessing. Dr. Hutson said, "I heard the message by Uncle Buddy called *The Second Blessing* from a taped recording someone made from an antique phonograph. He said, "I'm a Baptist and I don't believe in the second blessing, but after hearing Uncle Buddy, I said I have to have the second blessing." He was saying that Uncle Buddy was able to cross theological barriers and provoke him to a deeper walk with Jesus. How did Uncle Buddy do it? The absolute joy and contentment that radiated out of his life stirred people deeply everywhere he went. Surely the Lord will have a remnant on earth in this hour that will walk before him in true holiness. This remnant will provoke and stir the body of Christ to take off for the holy hill of God.

There is a verse in 1 Timothy, Chapter 6, that is so powerful but often overlooked because it is usually related to teaching on monetary matters. It is verse 6, *"But godliness with contentment is great gain."* This verse is dealing with lust and covetousness in the body. The apostle is saying that if we really want to have great gain, then we must be content and godly. We can see from the previous verse that even in that day, they evidently had some of the same prosperity teaching we have today. Verse 5 says, *"Perverse disputings of men of corrupt minds, and destitute of the truth, supposing that gain is godliness: from such withdraw thyself."* We have heard all too often from preachers of all denominations and doctrines that gain is godliness. This teaching hits us from every side. The Lord does want to bless His people, but He will not bless greed or covetousness. It is impossible to have contentment with those things in your heart. Trying to use the scripture against God Himself to fulfill the unsanctified desires of one's life is a gross error that is bringing anything but contentment in Christ. Even in this hour, the Lord has placed a holy grief in the hearts of many remnant Christians for those who have not found the true gain of godliness with contentment. When they speak out against the destruction caused by prosperity teaching, they are maligned and ostracized by many Christians. They are accused of having no faith and glorifying sickness or suffering. Much of the prosperity message makes a pitiful stab at substantiating itself by promoting a perverted view of scripture.

> ### *The dear Lord wants to place His desires in our heart.*

Psalm 37:4 says, *"Delight thyself also in the Lord; and He shall give thee the desires of thine heart."* This does not mean that if we praise and worship the Lord, He will give us everything we want. One preacher told me he had ordered a new car. I thought he meant that he had contacted a dealer and placed an order for the kind of car he wanted. I asked him when he expected the car and at what dealership he had made his purchase. He told me that the dealer was God and that he had ordered it on Psalm 37:4. He said, "I love the Lord and delight in Him and so I know He will give it to me." I said, "A new one?" He said, "Oh, yes, the Lord wants me to have the best." I found out later that he was polly-parroting a teacher of prosperity who taught people to expect such things, based on this misinterpretation and misrepresentation of Psalm 37:4. The verse means that when we are intimate with the Lord, He will provide us with the right desires. He will be the one who places the desires in our heart. Psalm 37:4 is a wonderful confirmation that the Lord can give us the mind of Christ as we seek His face. It is not a scripture to use to try to get God to give us a host of things that we do not really need.

Paul said in Philippians 4:11, *"For I have learned, in whatsoever state I am, therewith to be content."* He was content even in suffering, something not so common among Christians today. A constant association of the Gospel with glamour today almost makes us think that godliness is great gain. Godliness with contentment is great gain. Somehow the beloved apostle's beaten back just doesn't match up with a lot of so called Christianity in America. Paul walked in the salt covenant with the Lord Jesus, and the great joy he had could not have been produced by anything but trusting and obeying the Lord. The old songwriter knew true contentment when he penned the words, "Trust and obey for there is no other way to be happy in Jesus, but to trust and obey." Trusting is the bread and obeying is the salt. Again, it is simple, but profound. The problem is that true godly contentment is far too rarely found in the body of Christ.

> ### *There is a deep satisfaction of soul through walking in divine order.*

We visited a church where the pastor admittedly was not preaching personal holiness and separation from the world, which is simple obedience to Christ. He had many programs and activities, and the folks were ever so busy and well organized. But on their faces was a horrible emptiness that so grieved me that I wanted to scream out loud, "Where is the joy of the Lord? Why are your faces so empty? Where is the abundant life Jesus came to give us?" I wanted to say to this congregation, *"Who hath bewitched you, that you should not obey the truth?"* (Galatians 3:1) How can we think that the Lord will bless unrighteousness? Trying to have contentment outside of the covenants just won't work. How could a holy God ever place His countenance and radiation on open compromise and secret sin? The Lord loves righteousness. He is a holy God. In 1 Peter 1:16, the Bible says, *"Because it is written, be ye holy; for I am holy."* To walk in divine order and holy peace brings great satisfaction to the soul. To have the divine nature of God Himself in you, through the new birth, is the most wonderful of all the blessings man could have.

> ### *Maturity in Christ is allowing the Holy Ghost to inspect us daily.*

Paul said in 2 Corinthians 4:7, *"But we have this treasure in earthen vessels, that the excellency of the power may be of God, and not of us."* What could mankind ever receive that would in any way compare to the creator of the Universe living in him? Yet when that one that is indwelt by the creator continues to grieve the One who lives in him, it is great spiritual agony. The lack of salt in the believer simply equates with a presence of carnality. The presence of carnality grieves the Holy Ghost and brings holy despair to the real believer. A real Christian is grieved over any failure that the Holy Ghost points out to him, and an obedient Christian repents with a Godly sorrow. As we grow in the Lord, we soon find out the joy of allowing the Holy Ghost to inspect our hearts before the Lord.

When Jesus taught us the pattern for prayer in Matthew, Chapter 6, He gave us three different opportunities to inspect our hearts. You can't sincerely pray, *"Thy kingdom come and thy will be done,"* without a confrontation with anything not surrendered to His will. When we pray, *"Forgive us our debts as we forgive our debtors,"* we ask ourselves, "What do I need to have forgiven?" We ask, "Have I forgiven everyone who has wronged me?" This is a wonderful daily inspection. Then, when we pray, *"Deliver us from evil,"* there it is again, another inspection. Of course, the Master of prayer Himself knew what we needed to be victorious and content in Him. Wonderful, glorious, overflowing joy comes from being and staying right with our Redeemer.

I was visiting the powerful Times Square Church in New York. While waiting in the lobby for the service to start, I was talking with several people and inquiring as to how the services were going. I spotted a nice looking, clean cut, young Hispanic man with a beautiful glow on his face. I asked him how the meetings were going, and if he would describe them to me. He looked at me with a tear of joy filling the corner of each eye and said, "The Holy Ghost is uncovering every unholy thing in all of our lives." Then he said, "Isn't Jesus wonderful?" That is the salt covenant and the contentment therein. This young man wanted to walk with his loving Savior so closely that he welcomed every inspection of the Holy Ghost, so he could react with heartfelt repentance. No wonder he was totally vibrant with the touch of heaven!

> *Our heart should cry for the Lord to reveal everything offensive to Him.*

When we entered the service and began to worship with the believers there from all over the world, we saw a lot of folks with that same glow. I knew that the message there had the contents of the covenant of salt in it. They were preaching grace and personal holiness, bread and salt. The worship there seemed to be allowing expression of gratitude for the imputed righteousness they enjoyed. It was also a cry of the heart saying, "Lord, show me anything offensive to you, so I can adjust to your standard immediately." This is worshipping the Lord in the beauty of holiness. There is great contentment in Jesus. The sad thing is that so many Christians want to enter into great worship without allowing the Lord to do this sometimes painful operation of pinpointing and extracting the wrong and the carnal. Many modern church services are designed in a way that the Holy Spirit is never allowed opportunity to do this work. They are designed so by people who never allow the Holy Spirit to inspect and convict their lives. They futilely try to offer a sacrifice without salt. A certain death comes on their lives. Instead of having contentment with godliness, they have total despair.

Having pastored for many years, I have seen first hand the horrible frustration of the believer who is not walking in the salt covenant. I have seen the guilt, the anguish, the restlessness of heart, the constant open door the enemy has to attack and destroy. I have heard so much condemnation of condemnation. It is needless. If we are living right, we are not condemned. Of course, the devil is the accuser of the brethren. He wants to tempt us (which in itself is not a sin) and then condemn us for being tempted. However, if we give no place to the devil, he has nothing with which to condemn us, and his efforts to get us to live in defeat and guilt are cut off by those weapons which are not carnal.

> ## *Salt always makes people thirsty!*

Years ago, my wife and I operated a group home for troubled teenage girls. We took in these troubled delinquents from all over the state of Kentucky. The social workers would bring them to us in awful condition. Their lives were torn apart from abuse, drugs, alcohol, prostitution, the occult, and almost anything else one could name. We would tell them of the wonderful grace of Jesus, and they would get gloriously saved and delivered. We taught them to walk in holiness before the Lord, while trusting in His grace. They would just shine with the joy and contentment of the Lord. When the social worker would take them to the psychiatrist for evaluation and counseling, it would overwhelm the counselor. We knew this was happening and were waiting for the door to witness of the power of the gospel to the psychiatrist. Finally one day, the psychiatrist called the house. She said, "I just had to call and find out what it is that you are telling these girls.

They are so happy and full of life. I have to admit that they are radically changed." I proceeded to tell her of the power of the Lord to change a person's life when that person repents of sin and trusts His grace. I was careful to witness to her and let her know it wasn't my wife and I at all that had changed them. She had absolutely no ear for the gospel. She was just trying to find out from a counselor's point of view how to get the results she thought we were getting.

Finally she said to me, "For instance, what do you tell them is the reason they have feelings of guilt?" I said, "I tell them that the reason they have guilt feelings is because they are guilty. They have been bad girls, and they feel bad about their lives. The reason they have no more feelings of guilt is because they have been forgiven of those things they did and are not doing them any more." She said, "Oh, that is too simple. You must be sending them somewhere. It just can't work that way." These girls were tasting the joy of clean living while trusting the grace of God, and the world didn't know what to do with it. True holiness and true joy cannot be separated from each other. It is time that the world saw more of it. Salt always makes people thirsty.

> *There is immense joy in being completely right with God.*

We had an old preacher in our area named Bro. Cundiff, who walked in the salt covenant with the Lord. He was such a blessing to everyone. Wherever he went, he commanded such respect. He just glowed with the victory he had in Jesus. When I was a young preacher, he told me one day, "Son, live in such a way that if anyone says anything bad about you, they'll have to make it up." It was great advice. He wanted me to walk in the joy and contentment that he enjoyed. I believe that David was describing the same joy and contentment of holy living in Psalm 32. He states in verses 1 and 2, *"Blessed is he whose transgression is forgiven, whose sin is covered. Blessed is the man unto whom the Lord imputeth not iniquity, and in whose spirit there is no guile."* Here David is describing four levels of corruption in man: transgression, sin, iniquity, and guile. They are listed from the least to the greatest for emphasis, with guile being that deep rooted self-deception that comes from not dealing with the other three. David talks about the absolute joy of being completely right with God. Many have tried to use these verses in conjunction with the first half of Romans 8:1 mentioned earlier. However, David is not saying that he might do whatever he wants and the Lord will not charge sin to his life. He is diligent to tell us in the rest of the chapter of the horrible anguish of not being right with God and failing to confess his sin. Then, he elaborates on how he confessed and received this blessedness which he describes in verse 7 as *"songs of deliverance."* As a matter of fact, he wants to make sure that his testimony includes that there are many sorrows for the wicked, but the upright in heart can shout for joy.

> ## *There can be no contentment in carnality.*

All through the Bible it is there, plain and simple. Sin is what brings the cloud and the death. It is inevitable. We have so many courses and discourses in Christian circles that might as well be entitled, "How to Live Happy in Carnality." It is time the true holy remnant of imputed and personal righteousness rises up and shines forth in this perverse and wicked generation and shows the world what true joy is all about. An open heaven is still there and available to those who will walk in the Spirit and not fulfill the lusts of the flesh. They can walk in the contentment of Christ with which no cloud of oppression can compete.

After studying the salt covenant for years, I am convinced that the victory and power in the body of Christ is missing because of the absence of the salt covenant. When good salt is brought to the altar, the glory of the Lord starts to work. Don't bring the salt, and you will continue to live in condemnation, guilt, and spiritual confusion.

Paul dealt with sin in the church at Corinth very strongly in 1 Corinthians. When they repented and followed his counsel, he told them the results that came from their consent to do the right thing. In 2 Corinthians 7:11, Paul says, *"In all things ye have approved yourselves to be clear in this matter."* I assure you that there was joy in the Corinth camp when they read this letter. They were clear, clean, holy and full of godly zeal.

We had a brother from Tennessee come and preach at the local church I pastor. He had preached the night before and was actually only going to testify in the Sunday morning service. When I handed him the microphone, he greeted the people and told them how important it is to support their local church with their tithe and offerings. The more he talked about it, the stronger he got on the subject. He continued on the tithe and offering for quite some time. He blasted the congregation for not tithing, and like a carpenter he hammered and hammered on the matter until I felt that some of the congregation thought he and I had planned it. Over and over, in several different ways, he made his point.

I have never before and never since heard such a message on tithing. One thing I noticed as he nailed the subject was the difference in the countenance of the people in the congregation. The people who were slothful in this matter were sinking lower and lower in their seats. They were looking for relief from this modern Charles G. Finney. The people who were clear in the matter were sitting up straight and even saying, "Amen." They were untouched by the scathing message.

Forty-five minutes went by, and there seemed to be no end to the different directions this preacher could approach the subject of tithe and offerings. When he finally concluded, to my amazement, the Holy Spirit did many mighty spiritual works which had nothing to do with tithing among the people. I was really at a loss to understand it all. But one thing was sure, there was a noticeable difference between the ones who tithed and the ones who didn't. Some hurried on out with their hide burning, and I could hear some of the people tell one another, "I am sure glad I tithe." One brother said, "I'll be ready the next time someone preaches on tithing." Some of them told me later they really enjoyed the sermon. I went home with my head swimming, believing that the preacher had really heard from the Lord, but wondering what the congregation was thinking. I was deep in thought when I left the church.

> *The power of the Word will divide the pure from the impure.*

THE CONTENTMENT IN THE COVENANT

Like most pastors, later that day I found myself reliving the service and pondering on the what, how, and why of everything. It was then that the Lord showed me something very beautiful about what had taken place. I could see the division between the obedient and the disobedient. I could see the group with a cloud of guilt, and another group with a cloud of glory. In my spirit, I could see far beyond the issue of tithe and offerings. I could see far beyond our congregation, which for the most part welcomes the reproof of the Holy Ghost. I could see how the power of the Word would divide the pure and the impure. I could see the holy bride that was abiding in Him and not ashamed at His coming, while a host of foolish virgins twisted in nervous despair. I could see the ones who would not be cut with His two-edged sword because they were in line with the Word. These holy hill inhabitants, walking in sweet communion with the Lord, obedient to their Master, hating the spotted garment and loving the chastisement of the Lord are content in Christ, the bread of the covenant. The more the Word falls on this world, the brighter they will get. I could see how the glory of the Lord will fill the whole earth by the radiant open heaven relationship shining out of His covenant people. I could see how the true remnant church will fall in love so deeply with the Lord Jesus that every whim of His heart will be a shout of command to their soul. These saints will shine with His manifest presence. They are simply an army who trust and obey. I could see how all of the shallow teaching that leaves out personal holiness, or promotes it as a means of salvation, is going to be judged by the Word of God. I could see those who know their God shining brighter, and the ones walking in disobedience getting sicker and sicker.

The Lord made it so simple to me. The closer we get

to the end, the more the obedient remnant is going to shine with godly contentment and poise. Like the Hispanic boy at Times Square Church, with tears of joy they welcome the Master's reproof so they can better obey Him. This last day church, walking in the covenant of salt, will be settled in Him with such poise they will actually be glowing in the face of destruction, like the Moravians on the ship with John Wesley. They will have a contentment and confidence in Him that bears fruit wherever they go. The true peace will come from knowing that your sins are forgiven and that you're walking in holiness before Him, content in the covenant.

CHAPTER FOUR

THE POWER OF THE COVENANT

The remnant church is crying for the genuine power of the Holy Ghost to return to the church. It is a prayer that has become a cry of the soul. The precious Holy Spirit is praying through His yielded vessels with tenacity that often is just groaning which cannot be uttered. The Lord is pouring out the spirit of prayer on everyone who will accept it. The ones who are yielding to it are becoming literally jealous for the Lord. They detest the idea of a church or a man getting the glory that the Lord deserves. They want an explosion of God's power that will make it impossible for anyone to claim any glory. This kind of praying always precedes a great display of the power of God.

David prayed for the power and glory to come to the sanctuary in ways that he had seen in the past. He says in Psalm 63, "*O God, thou art my God; early will I seek thee: my soul thirsteth for thee, my flesh longeth for thee in a dry and thirsty land, where no water is; To see thy power and thy glory, so as I have seen thee in the sanctuary.*" Remember that David is one of the men in the Bible who prayed down fire. He knew about the power of God and would settle for nothing less than the real thing.

One of the major problems of our generation is that we have never seen a real outpouring of His power. Many of the intercessors who have the anointing to pray for the power of God have readily confessed that they really don't know what to expect when their prayer is answered. Some have come to me and said, "I'm not sure what to expect, but I am consumed with praying for it." Some of them have studied the moves of God in days gone by and have learned a little about what they are seeking.

> *The remnant church is getting desperate for the real power of God to come back to the church.*

I prayed with a dear Baptist preacher who said to the Lord, "Dear Lord, do something or take me on to heaven. I don't want to live here on this earth unless I see you move." He went on to tell the Lord how much glory He would get if He would bear his arm and shut the mouths of the scoffers by a display of His power. Another preacher was so bold as to tell the Lord with great distress of soul, "I can't stand to hear another prophecy of your great outpouring unless you let me see it with my own eyes." Preachers and laymen who at one time were content to talk about their denominations, churches, or some famous preacher are no longer talking that way. There is a deep growing realization that the Lord has already judged the one man flesh shows called ministry. The Hollywood imitating ministries who beg for money in order to finance their extravagant life styles are a far cry from the desperate cries of the interceding remnant who really wants to see the glory of the Lord. Desperate prayer like that of David in Psalm 63 is a necessary but expensive prerequisite of revival.

> ## *The Lord answers desperate prayer.*

Brother Leonard Ravenhill told me that the Lord doesn't answer prayer. The pause after this statement seemed much too long, but I could tell by those piercing eyes that there was more to follow. He finally finished by saying, "He answers desperate prayer." His statement caused me to travel back through my Christian life to check this out from my experiences. I told him I could not think of one instance in my entire Christian life that God didn't answer my prayer when it became desperate. Not one time has this kind of prayer gone unanswered. Brother Ravenhill went on to say that the reason men don't have the power of God is because they are willing to live without it. This is true. We must become desperate for the power of God to move again. Seeking the Lord and praying desperately causes at least two things to happen: First, The Lord will begin to reveal the changes we need to make in order to get into His divine pattern. Our Messianic friends have taught us well the Biblical truth that when the pattern is right, the glory falls. We seek the blessing, and He shows us how to get in line with His pattern so that we can receive it. The second thing is that the Lord will draw these praying saints to intimacy with Him, which will produce a fresh revelation of the deity of Christ. The shewbread, or the bread of His presence, is illuminated to us through the glory that falls because of our lining up with His pattern or covenants.

> ## *Bend the church and save the world.*

The great display of the power of the Holy Ghost in the Wales revival was in this same order. It began with the desperate cry of a young intercessor named Evans Roberts. He prayed, "Bend me." The cry of the revival later was, "Bend the church and save the world." A desperate person is willing to move from his place or condition in order to receive an answer to his prayer. The precious Holy Spirit taught Evans Roberts this though he didn't have great theological skills. All he knew was that *the effectual fervent prayer of a righteous man availeth much.* He allowed the Lord to bend him and move him into God's pattern; then the glory fell.   I firmly believe that Evans Roberts found himself walking in the covenant of salt. He had the bread, and he was willing to be the salt. He asked the Lord to bend him and make him good salt. He gave that salty life to the Lord as a sacrifice, and the rest is the history of one of the most awesome displays of God's glory the world has ever seen.

I was at a preacher's rally, and I was praying beside an older preacher. I overheard that seasoned minister praying for a religious group which in my opinion was outrageously wrong in their doctrine. I was taken aback by his prayer. I knew that he was a holiness preacher who lived a very separated and holy life. I was shocked because I thought he was compromising to pray a blessing on that group of people. It seemed to me that he was promoting their error. It bothered me so much that I asked him about it after the meeting. I approached him carefully, realizing that as a younger preacher I was much less experienced than he. I told him I couldn't help but notice that while we were praying for different ministries, he prayed for the Lord to bless a certain church that we both knew to be in gross error. I asked, "Do you think that is using spiritual wisdom?" He looked at me and said, "Son, you don't have to worry, the dear Lord won't bless sin or false doctrine. When I pray for the Lord to bless them I am praying for them to let Him move them to a place where He can bless them." I saw it very clearly.

> ## *We must allow the Lord*
> ## *to move us into the pattern.*

What I learned that night has helped me much down through the years in praying for the power of the Lord to come back to His church. Bless us by bending us. For example, praying for a blessing on finances is also a prayer for us to get to the place that the Lord can bless us financially. It is the same in any area of our lives. We are the ones who need to bend. We must give the Lord the license to move us into the pattern or covenant that will cause the glory to fall. The glory moves us into a place where He can impart great and fresh revelation of the Christ.

All true spiritual growth comes by and through the revelation of Christ to our hearts. As we move toward the Lord, He will direct us into the pattern that brings the glory and into the covenants that bring back the power of the Lord to the church. He is answering our prayer for power and blessing by revealing to us how to covenant with Him. His power never falls outside of His covenants. The prayer of desperation will take us to the covenants.

When the power of the Lord is released, it will manifest His glory, and the name of the Lord Jesus will be magnified. This power of His presence on His covenant people will be the means of evangelizing the world in the last day. We will see signs and wonders, but His presence will be much more important to the body than the miracles. Then, the miracles can occur and be in their proper order of priority.

When the genuine power of God falls on His people, it also illuminates the counterfeit. People are promoting meetings all over America as mighty moves of God, boasting of displays of God's power, with hardly a mention of repentance, holiness or the name of Jesus. These are fad-like waves moving through that only last a season, leaving all of its participants hollow and empty. They last only long enough to merchandise. There is a holy grief over the sham of so-called power in the church today. This holy grief intensifies in the people who are in desperate prayer for the genuine move of God.

> ### *Ishmael gets nervous when Isaac grows.*

The more this remnant prays the more nervous Ishmael is getting. He is getting dreadfully nervous. The more power Isaac gets, or the closer he gets to being weaned, the more uncomfortable Ishmael gets. The power of the antichrist is going to increase in the last days and deception is his sword. His deception will only stop when the Christ appears. Ishmael remains in the camp until Isaac is weaned. When Isaac is weaned, Ishmael has to go. The covenant is not with

Ishmael. The covenant people will prevail. The light shines on the true covenant people. Light has more power than darkness. All of the darkness in the world can not put out one little candle. However, darkness does not flee until light comes its way. The new covenant priesthood, walking in the power of God's covenants, will come and expose everything that is not genuine. The real power of God is coming to His real church, and all of the devils in hell can not stop it.

When Elijah stepped onto the stage at Mount Carmel before the false prophets of his day, he knew the only thing that would rid the land of the false was for the real to show up. He was so intent on glorifying the Lord that he poured twelve barrels of water on his sacrifice, so that no one but God could get it to burn. The false prophets of Baal were having a bad day because their god wouldn't answer them. Now, their day just got worse. The God of Elijah answered his prayer. The power of the Lord fell and brought much praise and glory to the Lord God of Israel. It also exposed all of the false prophets for what they really were.

The remnant church cries and pleads, not to have power for power's sake, but to have power so the Lord will be glorified and the devil will be terrified. This type of jealousy for the name of Jesus is touching the heart of the Lord. He put the cry in our hearts, and when we pray His heart with His heart, He will answer. But again, the answer comes by Him drawing us to His covenants so He can bless us.

> *The real power of God*
> *cannot fall outside His covenants.*

The covenants of the Lord have a great deal to do

with the coming outpouring. He is inviting His people to covenant with Him. The magnificent salt covenant gives the believer great power with the Lord. The justified soul living in personal righteousness carries a great deal of persuasion with the Lord. The book of James verifies that in Chapter 5, verse 16, *"The effectual fervent prayer of a righteous man availeth much."* Prevailing prayer is fervent and effectual, but it must come from a righteous man. This prayer must come from a man with imputed righteousness (bread) who is walking in personal righteousness (salt). This is the man who prays fervently and effectively. It is impossible to pray fervently with a cloud of guilt over your head, produced by a lack of personal holiness in your life. It is impossible to pray effectively with sin in your life. The Word makes this clear in Psalm 66:18, *"If I regard iniquity in my heart, the Lord will not hear me."*

The Lord wants so badly to show His children His mighty power. He is looking for that righteous one who puts salt on His bread and becomes a sacrifice unto Him. Then, He will reveal His mighty hand and release His power. We see this clearly in 2 Chronicles 7:14, the great verse that has become the prescription for revival prayer: *"If my people which are called by my name..."* That is the grace of God or the bread of the covenant. We are His people by His grace, called out by His power, and recipients of His grace. Now, here comes the salt: *"shall humble themselves, and pray, and seek my face, and turn from their wicked ways..."* This is personal righteousness, or the salt of the covenant. God has always honored the righteous, and He always will. He responds to the righteous. They have great power with the Lord in prayer. He continues, *"Then will I hear from heaven, and will forgive their sin and will heal their land."* That is a move of God.

He says in the next verse, *"Now mine eyes shall be open, and mine ears attent unto the prayer that is made in this place."* Now He looks, and now He hears. Why? Somebody brought some salt. That somebody was one of His, called by His name. When we bring the salt, our prayer gets powerful. Walking in the salt covenant releases the power of God in the believer. He has power with God and man.

> *The power of God*
> *is more than manifestations.*

The power of God is much more than spiritual manifestations in a meeting. It is really not the power of God we need, as much as power with God. That is the great need in the body. This is the wonderful part of the salt covenant. Great confidence in prayer makes powerful things happen, and great confidence in prayer comes from having a right relationship with the Lord. Power and persuasion with the Lord do not belong to those who love the world or to careless Christians who have no salt in their lives. Salt covenant people have power with God. He honors their requests. In John's gospel, we are told how the power of God is manifested through salty Christians, or Christians who are walking in personal righteousness. Jesus said in John 14:12, *"Verily, verily, I say unto you, He that believeth on me, the works that I do shall he do also; and greater works than these shall he do, because I go unto my Father."* This is a tremendous promise to the church.

Honest Christ-seeking Christians soon learn that every promise has a condition. Students of the Word who are being trained properly will automatically look for the condition as soon as they see the promise. One of the reasons the church is so weak today is that there has been too much emphasis on the promises and too little emphasis on the conditions. Jesus continued to emphasize the power of this promise in the next two verses: *"And whatsoever ye shall ask in my name, that will I do, that the Father may be glorified in the Son. If ye shall ask any thing in my name, I will do it."* Jesus could not have been any more emphatic. The next two verses bring us to the condition. *"If ye love me, keep my commandments. And I will pray the Father, and He shall give you another Comforter, that He may abide with you for ever."* He is saying, "Love me and do what I say and my power will be in you." The condition for such a powerful promise is spelled out for us simply and clearly. Jesus confirmed both the promise and condition again for us in John 15:7, *"If ye abide in me, and my words abide in you, ye shall ask what ye will, and it shall be done unto you."* Abiding in Him is the condition. Walking in the spirit is a walk of obedience. It is a walk of holiness and heart purity. This kind of living, while trusting in Him alone for redemption, has the power of God in it because the person who is abiding in Jesus has power with God. The Lord can trust that person who learns to abide. There really are people whom He can trust to have that blank check signed, and to whom He says, *"Whatever you ask, I will do it."* One would be foolish to think the Lord, in all of His wisdom, would grant that kind of power in prayer to one who is not walking in His presence. I am fully persuaded that the Lord is raising up many, even now, for these last days that he can entrust with great power and anointing. He has nurtured them and has taken them through His own school to prepare them for this hour. They are walking in the salt covenant, and they have the mind of Christ. They are being developed to the place of abiding. The fruit or power of this abiding will shake everything around it.

> ## God imparts great power and authority to those who abide in Him.

God turned the water works over to Elijah for three and one half years because He trusted him. Elijah knew it, and even said to Ahab, "It will not rain according to my word." Elijah came out of the wilderness, not to build a big ministry or promote himself in any way, but to deliver the Word of the Lord. God trusted him because in the wilderness Elijah had learned to abide in Him. He graduated from the seminary of solitude. This is the same school the Apostle Paul attended in Arabia.

We must learn to abide in Him. Then we will bear much fruit for the Lord Jesus. The Master taught us this process in John, Chapter 15. Beginning at verse one, He says, *"I am the true vine, and my Father is the husbandman. Every branch in me that beareth not fruit He taketh away: and every branch that beareth fruit, He purgeth it, that it may bring forth more fruit."* We see three positions on bearing fruit that are mentioned by the Master. First, we see no fruit. Next, we see the branch that bears fruit, and then we see how that branch bears more fruit. He takes away that which has no fruit. He purges that which has fruit, that it may have more fruit. Certainly, we are grafted into the vine by the grace of God, and every true born again Christian ought to bear fruit. Jesus wants us to be productively powerful, so He purges (or sanctifies) us so we can produce more fruit. But we shouldn't stop there. The Lord goes on to teach us the power of abiding in Him. He says in verse 5, *"I am the vine, ye are the branches. He that abideth in me, and I in him, the same bringeth forth much fruit."* We now see *much fruit*, which is a higher level of productivity. This comes as a result of abiding. First, we bear fruit, and after purging we bear more fruit, then we bear much fruit when we abide in Him. How do we abide in Him? Jesus gives us the answer in verse 10, *"If ye keep my commandments, ye shall abide in my love; even as I have kept my Father's commandments, and abide in His love."*

> # *The Salt Covenant produces productive power.*

There is productive power in holy living. The salt covenant is the covenant of holiness, responsibility, and productivity. God is a holy God. The Holy Ghost breathed on holy men of God to give us the Holy Scriptures, which make us wise unto salvation; therefore, we can go to a holy city, where the holy creatures cry holy, holy, holy before the holy angels around His holy throne. The complaint against the fiery Methodist evangelist, Sam Jones, was, "Every time you open your Bible, you preach on holiness." As he held up his Bible, he answered, "I don't even have to open it. It says right here on the cover, Holy Bible."

We can not covenant with a holy God without personal holiness, and we can have no power outside of His covenants. There is no teaching I fear on earth more than the teachings that put more emphasis on power than on holiness. Another teaching I fear is that of holiness without grace. God's power rests on people who are wearing the imputed righteousness of God <u>and</u> walking in personal righteousness before Him. This is the salt covenant.

The great prophet Elisha kept passing by the house of the lady from Shunem. She told her husband one day, "I perceive this to be a holy man of God." No higher compliment could have been paid this prophet. The power of God was all over him. He spoke the word, and the Shunemite woman who had no child brought forth a child. Miracles flowed out of his life everywhere he went. He had the anointing that identified him as a holy man of God. Oh, for the church to have that flavor again! True holiness that radiates on the countenance of God's covenant people will bring conviction on sinners and backsliders.

It was the holy fire of God on the faces and in the voices of Paul and Silas that brought the Philippian jailer to them, broken and repentant, crying, "What must I do to be saved?" That is the power of God at work. People want that kind of anointing, they say, but not desperately enough to take the persecution and to live separated from the world. Christians, for the most part, aren't standing up to claim the promise in 2 Timothy 3:12, *"Yea, and all that will live Godly in Christ Jesus shall suffer persecution."* Yet, without living Godly there can be no holy fire. We accept and understand that there can be no remission of sin without the shedding of blood, but we can't seem to understand or accept that without the shedding of flesh there can be no real revival. The Philippian jailer ran into two mighty men of God. He knew they had something in their lives that he didn't have. He heard the singing in the prison. He saw the power of God at work, and he was convinced that he needed what they had.

THE POWER OF THE COVENANT

> ## *Salt Covenant people convince sinners by the principal of seeing and hearing.*

It takes the power of God in our lives to convince sinners of their sin and prove to them that the power of God is greater than the power of darkness. The jailer heard and saw. These are the two things that drive a truth home to the souls of men. When an individual both sees and hears, he receives it into his spirit. This is why Jesus did not send anyone out to preach the Gospel without giving them the power to do miracles. He did this so the hearers of the message could also see the work of God through the miracles. In Acts 20:20, Paul says that he has both shown and taught his listeners. They could hear Paul preach it and see him live it. In the verses that follow, Paul rehearses the manner of holiness that he has lived before the people.

The powerful Sanhedrin Council commanded the early apostles not to teach or to preach at all in the name of Jesus. Their answer was, *"For we cannot but speak the things which we have seen and heard."* The apostle John said in 1 John 1:1, *"That which was from the beginning, which we have heard, which we have seen with our eyes..."* The principal of seeing and hearing is very plain in the Scripture. This is why the salt covenant is so important, because personal righteousness can be seen by everyone. Salt covenant people are not just talking it; they are also walking it.

The principal of seeing and hearing is also used by the dark powers to destroy lives. The enemy wants people to see and hear things that will extirpate godliness. This is why the devil is so proud of his movie and video business. The wickedness can both be seen and heard. It is so sad that the number one passion of Americans is audio and video entertainment, seeing and hearing what is for the most part produced by hell itself. The things many Christians allow in their homes in the name of entertainment are totally shocking. Many people pay for this entertainment to be delivered to them, which is nothing less than demonic forces driving wickedness into their hearts through the avenues of seeing and hearing. This is how Lot vexed his soul. In 2 Peter 2:8 it has this to say about Lot, *"For that righteous man dwelling among them, in seeing and hearing, vexed his righteous soul from day to day with their unlawful deeds."* The power of seeing and hearing is the very reason the devil works so hard to get men of God to compromise. Once he succeeds in causing them to stumble, he points struggling souls to them and says, "He is preaching one thing and doing another." The devil points no one to a holy man of God. He tries to keep souls from coming in contact with salt covenant people. The dark world knows very well what works in the kingdom of God. One demon screamed out, "Jesus I know and Paul I know." The dark world feared that holy man because he had power with God. Paul said in 1 Corinthians 2:4, *"And my speech and my preaching was not with enticing words of man's wisdom, but in demonstration of the Spirit and of power."* His influence cost the dark world every time he moved.

> ## *A lack of salt is a lack of genuine power with God.*

A person said to me once that a certain preacher who had

fallen now has no influence. I said to him, "If only you were right about that." I went on to explain that the fallen preacher still has influence, but for the wrong side. Everyone has influence, but far too many Christians and ministers have no influence for the good. They have no salt. Some ministries, as well as some entire denominations, have backed away from personal holiness and compromised with the world. They have lost their power with God and their persuasion with men. Eventually they will wind up in the same ecclesiastical scrap pile as all the rest who lost their salt. They have no power, no influence, and no fruit.

When I was a child, my parents would let me go to the service station that was close to our house to get a soft drink or candy bar. A lot of times, there would be several men standing around, talking and trading. I would listen to them curse and talk vulgar, even though I knew my parents wouldn't approve of this. They seemed to be unconcerned that I was listening or that it might have an adverse effect on me. However, there was one man who stopped in the service station from time to time who would put a halt to their wicked talk. It was an old Methodist preacher who lived in our community. His name was Brother Hobart Miller. He was just a frail little man, but when he came up to that crowd of ruffians, there was an instant change in their conversation. Each of them would greet Brother Hobart and shake his hand. The whole atmosphere changed in that little service station. Brother Hobart attended the same Methodist church my parents and I did. I had heard him pray. When they called on him to pray, he would get out of the pew, kneel down, and proceed to shake the heavens and the earth. I remember thinking that I had not seen any of those men at church, but they seemed to know what a connection Brother Hobart had with the Lord. As a child I was amazed at the influence that this holy man of God had on this rough crowd. I realize now that Brother Hobart had salt in his life. I have often relived that scene at the little gas station and cried unto God for some salty Christians who would have the same effect on our schools, government offices, and even our churches as Brother Hobart had on those men at the station.

When I see some of the light entertaining ministers today, working their crowds with manipulative speech that is terribly void of the power of God, it causes a holy grief to come up in my soul. The reason that these entertainers have so much counterfeit manifestation in their meetings is because after their speeches, they just can't stand to see nothing happen, so they make it happen. The genuine power of God is not going to honor compromising carnality, so they resort to all kinds of trickery and tactics to appear credible. The remnant church is appalled at all of this because they have the heart of Christ, and they identify with His grief in this matter.

While the entertainers are rejoicing over their exaggerated results, the Hannahs are praying in a Samuel to take the place of Eli. The corrupt priesthood of Eli continued to operate even though the Bible says in 1 Samuel 3:1, *"There was no open vision."* The reason the Word was precious or scarce in those days is that Eli, the priest, was living in sin and compromise. He allowed sin to flourish all around him and brought the standard of morality in Israel to an all time low. He had no power with God or man. He lost his salt, and the judgment of the Lord was upon him. He was going through all of the motions, but he was totally ineffective. Eli knew very well that this boy Samuel, who stayed in the presence of the Lord, had a word for him that wasn't good. I believe he became increasingly aware of that as Samuel grew. The real thing has to show up in order for the counterfeit to be revealed. Samuel walked in holiness before the Lord, and none of his words fell to the ground. We certainly can't live like Eli and have the results of Samuel. Loss of salt equals loss of power.

> *Shaven Samson is a type*
> *of the powerless church*
> *living outside of the Salt Covenant.*

Living outside the salt covenant is like Samson after his hair was cut. He jumped up to do great exploits, as he had in the past, but his power was gone. Samson said in Judges 16:20, *"I will go out as at other times before, and shake myself." The last part of that verse says, "And he wist not that the Lord was departed from him."* This is a sad but true type of a lot of saltless ministries of our day.

A spokesman for a major denomination was lamenting the loss of membership and respect in America. The spokesman cited several different possible reasons for the decline; however, there was not one mention of the wholesale compromise with the world. There was not even a hint of recognizing the real problem, which is the loss of salt. There are several denominations in America that were born out of holiness revivals. The meetings were anointed and Christ centered. The hearts of men were brought under great conviction by the power of the Holy Ghost. They had salt, and they had power. The result was genuine conversions, changed communities, great harvest, and the fear of God falling on everyone around them.

The Sheriff in the county of Rome, New York confessed to falling under great conviction when he was about four miles from where the great meetings were held in the days of Charles G. Finney. He said, "As I pulled my buggy on the little bridge outside of Rome, a strange feeling came over me. I found myself weeping. Being a rather stout man and not given to emotions, I wondered at it all. Upon my arrival in Rome, I found that the whole town was in the same state as myself. My anxious heart found a place to pray and repent of all of my ungodliness." That is the power and the fire of God. When that kind of power is moving, you can expect to find some folks who are in the blood covenant who have entered into the great salt covenant.

When I review many of the old hymns, I can see the salt covenant so clearly. General William Booth, the founder of the Salvation Army, penned the words to the famous song, *"Send the Fire."* The words of the song are a cry for the power of God to fall, but it is also a clear call to holiness. One portion of the song says, "The power to walk this world in white; send the fire today." We are beginning to hear this message in some of the songs of our day. The call to heart purity and intimacy with Jesus is coming from the remnant church songwriters. Some of these songs sound as if they were written by Wesley or Finney. The testimony of the old saints who walked in holiness before the Lord is ringing out again. The power always accompanies the people of the salt covenant. We can see this so clearly as we look again at 2 Chronicles, Chapter 13. Abijah is fearless as he stands before Jeroboam. In the face of the battle, outnumbered two to one, Abijah doesn't flinch. Abijah understood the power of the salt covenant, and before they day was over, Jeroboam understood it as well. Abijah cited the salt covenant in verse 4 as the reason Jeroboam better leave them alone. Abijah could not have stood without fear in the face of these idolaters had there not been the presence of the power of the Lord.

> # *Walking in the Salt Covenant brings the fear of God on the world.*

Jacob could not have made a safe return to Bethel had there not been a revival of personal holiness before he and his company began their journey. In Genesis 35, beginning at verse 2, we read, *"And Jacob said unto his household, and to all that were with him, Put away the strange gods that are among you, and be clean, and change your garments: And let us arise and go up to Bethel; and I will make there an altar unto God, who answered me in the days of my distress, and was with me in the way which I went. And they gave unto Jacob all of the strange gods that were in their hand, and all their earrings which were in their ears; And Jacob hid them under the oak which was by Shechem. And they journeyed: and the terror of God was upon the cities that were round about them, and they did not pursue after the sons of Jacob."* This is the amazing power of God that falls around the people of God who walk before Him in personal holiness.

Jacob was in the *"everlasting covenant."* In his loins was the Messiah Himself, the very bread of life, but he was not walking in the salt covenant. Jacob knew the grace of God had been with him and that he had experienced a measure of blessing and divine protection. He needed to go up to another level and knew how to do it. He was aware of the idolatry in his camp. He knew that if he expected the Lord to honor him with a new level of power and protection, he would have to honor the Lord by putting away every known sin and failure. He demanded personal holiness from himself and his entire household, and the Lord moved on his behalf. Evidently a wall of fire and anointing was on this little traveling band. The powerful nations couldn't touch Jacob or his herds as he walked through their midst. God's power falls when the pattern is right. The salt covenant is the right pattern and order in which the children of God are to walk. As a recipient of God's grace, Jacob put personal holiness to work, and the glory fell.

> *A small remnant walking in the covenant has power over great armies.*

The answer is not in the number of people or in military might. It only takes a remnant that is living right to bring the victory. When Jacob answered the call of God to go back to Bethel, he honored his jealous God and put away from him and his household every false god and every worldly attraction. God honored this with a divine presence that caused a terror among the nations.

Gideon's little army of three hundred men was just too much for the host of the Medianites. Before that historical battle, there was an evening of idol bashing throughout the town. Like Jacob, Gideon got rid of the idols around him as soon as he was called to the battle. Gideon then organized an army of 32,000 men to fight the Medianites. Even though this was just a few compared to his enemies, the Lord trimmed it down. He showed Gideon how to get rid of the cowards, then how to get rid of the careless. The remnant left was 300 men. The Lord used these 300 men to defeat the Medianites. It is the method in which he used them that fascinates me. They each had a trumpet and a vessel with a light in it. At Gideon's signal, this little band of 300 men was to blow their trumpets and break their vessels so that the light would shine out. They had nothing that would be classified as a weapon of war, but for the remnant that wrestles with principalities and powers, what they had is significant.

The vessel with light in it represents the children of God who are indwelt by the Holy Spirit. The broken vessel represents consecration. The light shining out of the broken vessel is a type of the power of the Holy Spirit flowing out of a consecrated and holy vessel. The trumpet is the Word of God, and the shout is the shout of faith that overcomes the world. The outcome of this battle displays the power of God that moves through the overcoming saints who are walking in personal holiness. There is no power in the trumpet blast if there is no light in the vessel. No one can see the light in the vessel if the vessel isn't broken. Again, the pattern was right, and the enemy suffered heavy loss. The power of God puts fear and confusion in the devil's camp. The Medianites were soundly defeated by just a small remnant.

John Wesley said he could change England if the Lord would give him a hundred men who feared nothing but God and hated nothing but sin. Wesley knew the power of the covenant. God gave him the men, and England was changed. Wesley didn't ask for a thousand men. He asked for a hundred men who were right with God. He knew his God would pour out His power on the ones who were walking in personal holiness, while resting in the grace of God. The Lord hasn't changed. He never will. The power of the salt covenant is still the same.

CHAPTER FIVE

THE COVENANT AND THE PRIESTHOOD

E verything the Lord does to men and for men, He does it through His priesthood. There has never been a major move of God that was not preceded by the correcting of the priesthood. Samuel came forth to correct the priesthood of Eli. Zadok moved in where Abiathar was. Caiaphas and Annas were high places that had to be brought low by the real high priest, John the Baptist. It is a pattern that we can plainly see throughout the Old and New Testaments. Therefore, it is imperative for us to understand the priestly part of our relationship with the Lord in the salt covenant. It may be noted in both Leviticus 2:13 and Numbers 18:19 that it is the priest with whom the salt covenant is made. The Lord has never authorized anyone except the priesthood to put the salt on the sacrifice. Ezekiel 43:24 states, *"And thou shalt offer them before the Lord, and the priest shall cast salt upon them."*

The Covenant and the Priesthood

> ### *Only priest could put salt on the sacrifice.*

When Jesus said in Mark 9:49 that *"every one shall be salted with fire and every sacrifice shall be salted with salt,"* there is no question that He was referring to the covenant of salt. He went on to say to them that they should have salt in themselves, referring to personal holiness. In a spiritual sense, He was authorizing Jews of every tribe to put salt on the sacrifice. In the old covenant, this was reserved only for the tribe of the Levites. Either the Lord has dropped the standard of the covenant, or He is raising all of His disciples to the office of the priest. Of course, the latter is true. It is evident in the Scriptures that the twelve disciples were not all of the tribe of Levi. And Jesus Himself, our high priest, was of the tribe of Judah, a non-priestly tribe.

The Lord is not changing His standard. He never does. He is raising up to Himself a spiritual priesthood that fulfills the Levitical order and goes far beyond it so that the whole kingdom of God becomes a priesthood. This kingdom of priests includes even the Gentiles, who are no blood kin to any of the tribes of Israel, certainly not the Levites. This kingdom of priests on earth is, of course, His church. The Bible clearly teaches that the recipients and the participants of the new covenant are, in fact, a priesthood.

In Revelation 1:5 and 6, we find these words: *"And from Jesus Christ, who is the faithful witness, and the first begotten of the dead, and the prince of the kings of the earth. Unto Him that loved us, and washed us from our sins in His own blood, And hath made us kings and priests unto God and His Father; to Him be glory and dominion for ever and ever. Amen."* The Word here is telling us that the washed in the blood saints are kings and priests (translated a kingdom of priests) unto the Most High God.

> # *The blood washed saints of God are the Royal Priesthood.*

The old covenant priests had to be the right bloodlines, and they had to be washed in a ceremonial cleansing before they began the work of the priesthood. The new covenant priesthood has to be washed in the blood of the King who was and is our high priest in order to be a part of the kingdom of priests. That is why it is referred to in 1 Peter 2:9 as a *Royal Priesthood. "But ye are a chosen generation, a royal priesthood..."*

In Revelation 5:9-10 we find these words: *"And they sung a new song, saying, Thou art worthy to take the book, and to open the seals thereof: for thou wast slain, and hast redeemed us to God by thy blood out of every kindred, and tongue, and people, and nation; and hast made us unto our God kings and priests: and we shall reign on the earth."* Again, we see the redemption by the blood of Jesus actually conferring people of every tribe, Jew and Gentile, into a royal priesthood, or a kingdom of priests. Also in Revelation 20:6, there is a confirmation that this royal priesthood will reign with Christ in the millennium. His whole body is actually a kingdom of priests. This is why in the New Testament we find the apostle, the prophet, the evangelist, the pastor, and the teacher, but there is no mention of the priest. All of the redeemed of the Lord are priests unto the Most High God. Every washed in the blood saint is a part of the glorious priesthood of God on earth, regardless of tribe, tongue or kindred. Through the right blood and the right washing, we have the priesthood conferred upon us by the high priest Himself, Jesus Christ. Jesus is a high priest forever after the order of Melchisedec, which is a higher pre-existent priesthood than the Levitical order. The whole theme of the book of Hebrews is that the priesthood of Jesus is greater than that of the Levitical order. The Levitical order was earthly and only a shadow or type of the eternal and spiritual priesthood that is after the order of Melchisedec.

The order of Melchisedec

We first see this priesthood of Melchisedec in the book of Genesis, Chapter 14, verse 18: *"And Melchisedec king of Salem brought forth bread and wine: and he was the priest of the most high God."* This mysterious appearing of Melchisedec has been the focus of much theological debate down through the ages. Many Bible scholars have had controversy among themselves over just who this Melchisedec really was. We know from this initial appearance that he was a king and a priest of the Most High God. In Hebrews 7:3 we find a more detailed description of him: *"Without father, without mother, without descent, having neither beginning of days, nor end of life; but made like unto the Son of God; abideth a priest continually."* The priesthood of Melchisedec is a perpetual, pre-existent, and powerful priesthood. Melchisedec manifests himself to Abraham as he returns from the slaughter of the kings. He furnishes both the bread and the wine at their meeting, and then pronounces a blessing that is certainly appropriate for such a powerful priesthood. Melchisedec says to Abraham in Genesis 14:19, *"Blessed be Abram of the most high God, possessor of heaven and earth:"* That blessing is about as powerful as can be given, and the words of it are very significant when we see it in the light of the royal priesthood that will reign on the earth, mentioned in Revelation 20:6.

After the blessing, Abraham pays Melchisedec his tithe and they part company. He who was a king and a priest and yet in the loins of Abraham was both the tribe of Levi, which would bring forth the Levitical priesthood, and the tribe of Judah, which is the tribe of the king. I firmly believe that the priesthood of Melchizedek was transferred to Abraham at this meeting for a time known as the old covenant. In other words, the pre-existent, continual priesthood became temporal and earthly until the time that Messiah, who is a priest forever after the order of Melchisedec, would come. A powerful Messianic utterance plainly stating this truth concerning the coming Messiah is found in Psalm 110:4: *"The Lord hath sworn, and will not repent, Thou art a priest forever after the order of Melchisedec."* We know that this is speaking of Jesus because the book of Hebrews refers to this prophecy and plainly states that it is Jesus the Christ. Hebrews 6:20 states, *"Even Jesus, made a high priest forever after the order of Melchisedec."*

> ## *The Melchisedec priesthood follows Messianic pattern.*

I believe that the appearing of Melchisedec to Abraham was one of the many appearances of the pre-carnate Christ in the Old Testament. The priesthood of Melchisedec follows the exact pattern of the Messiah. Melchisedec, perpetual and pre-existent, became a human priesthood in the Levitical order for a season of time, only to return in power to that which is spiritual and heavenly. Jesus, the eternal and pre-existent creator, became a man in the fullness of the Godhead bodily (Col. 2:9) to redeem mankind. His ministry became human, but He will come back again in the fullness of His deity as the King of kings and Lord of lords.

John 1:10 states, *"He was in the world, and the world was made by Him, and the world knew Him not."* They did not understand His pre-existence. They desired to stone Him for His profession of pre-existence in John 8:58, when He said, *"Verily, verily, I say unto you, Before Abraham was, I am."* John could plainly see the pre-existence of the Lord Jesus and started his first epistle by stating, *"That which was from the beginning, which we have heard, which we have seen with our eyes, which we have looked upon, and our hands have handled, of the Word of life."* When Jesus made the statement in John 8:56, *"Your father Abraham rejoiced to see my day; and he saw it and was glad,"* He could have been referring to His meeting with Abraham through Melchisedec. It would certainly fit the Bible pattern.

Jesus made several comments concerning His pre-existence, though it seemed the people could not see it. There is no doubt that Jesus is the King of kings and the great High Priest forever. Most Messianic Jews can see the pattern clearly by their acquaintance with Judaism. The transfer of the priesthood from Levi back to the spiritual priesthood after the order of Melchisedec is something even orthodox Jews believe will happen. Jews who reject Jesus as the Messiah are expecting this priestly transfer to be made by Messiah when He comes, based upon the prophecies concerning the order of Melchisedec. Sadly, they are blinded to the fact that the transfer has already been made, and that Jesus the Messiah was actually conferred by the Levitical order as the high priest. The book of Hebrews calls Him "the great high priest."

> # *The baptism of Jesus*
> # *was a priestly baptism.*

When the new covenant appears, we should look for the transfer back from Abraham to Melchisedec, or should we say from Levi back to the perpetual, pre-existent priesthood. This is actually what happened in the Jordan River at the baptism of Jesus. Jesus told John at His baptism, recorded in Matthew 3:15, *"For thus it becometh us to fulfill all righteousness."* Every tenet of the Levitical law for the conferring of the priesthood was fulfilled right here in the water of the Jordan River. Jesus needed no baptism of repentance, for He was perfect. He did not submit to water baptism just so we would see the need for it, as some suppose. The baptism of Jesus was to fulfill all righteousness. Jesus received a priestly baptism by a Levitical priest. This is when the transfer of the priesthood occurred, and that is why the heavens opened and the voice of God uttered. Jesus was thirty years old, which is the age for the high priest to begin his ministry. He was ceremonially washed or baptized by the only man in the world who was qualified to do so. John the Baptist was the real high priest of Israel. We think of him as a prophet, and certainly he was, but Jesus said John was more than a prophet. Jesus said in Luke 7:26, *"A prophet? Yea, I say unto you, and much more than a prophet."* Was John Aaronic? Was he the firstborn son? Did his ministry begin at age thirty? Was he in the covenant of salt of personal holiness? Yes, yes. He had the credentials. God had raised him up for this very purpose, to fulfill all righteousness.

Even John the Baptist's mother, Elisabeth, was pure Aaronic. Luke 1:5-7 states, *"There was in the days of Herod, the king of Judea, a certain priest named Zacharias, of the course of Abia: and his wife was of the daughters of Aaron, and her name was Elisabeth. And they were both righteous before God, walking in all of the commandments and ordinances of the Lord blameless. And they had no child, because that Elisabeth was barren, and they were both now well stricken in years."* The Lord was very careful to fulfill every tenet of the law for the priesthood in preparation for the transfer of the priesthood from the Levitical order back to the order of Melchisedec. Under the Levitical order, every high priest had to be of the lineage of Aaron. Aaron was of the tribe of Levi, but was born some 400 years after Levi. That means there were a lot of Levites who where not Aaronic, but no descendants of Aaron who were not Levites. There could be no high priest except of the lineage of Aaron. Aaron's sons made more priests from the tribe of Levi, but the high priesthood was reserved for pure Aaronic stock.

> *We see the Lord
> purifying the priesthood.*

By the time Jesus appeared, the office of the high priest in Israel had become a political office, with a new high priest elected each year. It was totally corrupt, as we can see in their dealings with Jesus. Again, God's pattern is that He corrects the priesthood before He moves mightily. We could say, when we see the Lord purifying the priesthood, that something major is about to happen. The Lord would not allow the corrupt priesthood of Caiaphas to perform any duty of righteousness on the Messiah. Rest assured that there would be no other than Aaronic hands laid on Jesus at His baptism. The Lord prepared carefully the vessel He would use to confer the Levitical order back to the order of Melchisedec. John the Baptist walked in holiness before the Lord, as did his parents. The Bible makes it very clear that they were walking in the covenant of the Lord. The real high priest of Israel was not in the synagogue nor in some political office, and certainly not in total spiritual blindness. The real high priest of Israel was crying in the wilderness. The anointing was all over John the Baptist, while the corrupt political priesthood of the religious system of Israel had nothing but ritual.

Perfect order

The people flocked to hear John preach. This "more than a prophet" salt preacher was scathing dead religion and preaching holiness. He was telling them of the One to come who would baptize with fire and the Holy Ghost. He was in the spirit of Elijah and a powerful preacher of righteousness, but he was also the bonafide high priest of Israel, carefully picked and produced of God for the fulfilling of the law of righteousness concerning the priesthood. The firstborn son of a son and a daughter of Aaron who began his ministry at thirty years of age, walking in a covenant of separation, or salt, baptizes or ceremonially cleanses a firstborn son of a daughter of Judah, the kingly tribe, who is also thirty years of age. This put the king and the priest back together, which is what Melchisedec was, a king and a priest. It is all in perfect order. Hebrews 7:14-17 states, *"For it is evident that our Lord sprang out of Juda; of which tribe Moses spake nothing concerning priesthood. And it is yet far more evident: for that after the similitude of Melchisedec there ariseth another priest, who is made, not after the law of a carnal commandment, but after the power of an endless life. For He testifieth, Thou art a priest forever after the order of Melchisedec."*

Everything was in perfect and divine order. John's priesthood was ready to decrease as explained carefully in the priestly terms in Acts 13:25, *"And as John fulfilled his course..."* and the pre-existent, perpetual priesthood of the great high priest was ready to increase. As the actual transfer took place, all three manifestations of the Godhead gave witness. Jesus stood in the water; the Holy Ghost fell on Him in the form of a dove, and the voice of the Father in heaven said, *"This is my beloved Son in whom I am well pleased."* What an awesome moment! Is it any wonder that Jesus said of John, *"born of women there hath not risen a greater."* The priesthood was transferred from Melchisedec to Abraham, Abraham to Levi, Levi to Aaron, Aaron to John the Baptist, and John to Jesus Christ the great eternal high priest after the order of Melchisedec.

One of the duties of a Levitical high priest was to make other priests through ceremonial cleansing. John said, *"I indeed baptize you with water,"* but the great high priest, Jesus, will baptize with the Holy Ghost, thus making spiritual priests. Paul refers to this in 1 Corinthians 12:13, *"For by one*

Spirit are we all baptized into one body," and that body is a kingdom of priests. Of course, Paul is referring to the new birth. All are baptized by the same high priest, who is also a king, making it *a "royal priesthood."* We should wonder no more why the redeemed, washed in the blood saints are called kings and priests. We are peculiar. We are different from any other group on the face of the earth.

Only priests can eat the bread.

Under the old covenant, only the priests could eat the shewbread. In the new covenant priesthood, as well, only the priests can eat the bread. But we are the priests, made so in divine and perfect order, fulfilling every ordinance of God's law. Jesus said in Mark 14:22, *"Take eat, this is my body."* The psalmist said in Psalm 34:8, *"O taste and see that the Lord is good."* In the old covenant, only the priests could put salt on the sacrifice. Tradition tells us that the priests carried a salt bag on their belts under their prayer shawl for that purpose. Every sacrifice had to have salt on it. Likewise, in the new covenant, only the priests can put salt on the sacrifice. All the redeemed of the Lord from every tribe and nation make up the new covenant priesthood. We are to put salt on the sacrifice. Jesus is the bread, or the sacrifice, and we are the salt that goes on the bread. No one else but the priest is eligible to put the salt on the sacrifice.

There are many religions that practice personal righteousness and good morality. There are many groups who live strict and disciplined lives. Unless they have been baptized by the Spirit into the body of Christ by the new birth, they are not in the priesthood. Therefore, their salt is no good. All of their good works is salt without savor, good for nothing but to be trodden under the foot of man. The kingdom of priests must be the ones who put on the salt. This royal priesthood is able to go on into the holy of holies, or spiritual fullness, and put salt on the bread. We find in Hebrews 10:19-22, that our sure access to the holy place is beautifully spelled out for us in priestly terms of purification. *"Having therefore, brethren, boldness to enter into the holiest by the blood of Jesus, By a new and living way, which He hath consecrated for us, through the veil, that is to say, His flesh; And having a high priest over the house of God; Let us draw near with a true heart in full assurance of faith, having our hearts sprinkled from an evil conscience, and our bodies washed with pure water."*

The King — the Priest — the Covenant

Hebrews 4:16 says, *"Let us therefore come boldly unto the throne of grace, that we may obtain mercy, and find grace to help in time of need."* We enjoy all the things that only priests of God can enjoy because we have been made priests unto God by the blood of Jesus, He that has the pre-existent, perpetual priesthood after the order of Melchizedek.

As stated earlier, both in Leviticus 2:13 and Numbers 18:19, it is evident that the salt covenant was for the priesthood. In 2 Chronicles 13, we find that one of the reasons for the sure victory for Abijah is that they had the correct priesthood and were walking in the salt covenant. It is a priesthood covenant. We are a royal priesthood. When that royal priesthood walks in personal holiness and righteousness before the Lord, no weapon formed against them will prosper. When we say that God doesn't move until he corrects the priesthood, we are actually saying that the priests have to be in the salt covenant. The familiar verse in I Peter 4:17, *"For the time is come that judgment must begin at the house of God,"* is a reference to this pattern. He first deals with His priests.

In 2 Chronicles 29, we find the account of a great move of God in Israel. Hezekiah was installed as king at the age of 25, at a time of great spiritual poverty in Israel. In the first month of the first year, he opened the temple doors and called for the Levites. He gave them these instructions in verse 5, *"Hear me, ye Levites, sanctify now yourselves, and sanctify the house of the Lord God of your fathers, and carry forth the filthiness out of the Holy Place."* He goes on to tell them the reason they are in such a condition as a nation. He points out their sins and backsliding with great accuracy and a deep burden for his people. Notice he is addressing the priesthood. It is evident that King Hezekiah knew God's pattern of correcting the priesthood as a prerequisite for revival. It is the priests who were commanded to carry forth the filth out of the Holy Place. Personal holiness, or the salt of the covenant, is really what Hezekiah is demanding from the priesthood.

> ## *The king calls them back to the Covenant.*

Notice Hezekiah uses the term *covenant* in verse 10. He said, *"Now it is in mine heart to make a covenant with the Lord God of Israel, that His fierce wrath may turn away from us."* We have to get back to the covenant of the Lord. The priests were stirred up, and they went to work. We read in verses 15 and 16, *"And they gathered their brethren, and sanctified themselves, and came, according to the commandment of the king, by the words of the Lord, to cleanse the house of the Lord. And the priests went into the inner part of the house of the Lord, to cleanse it, and brought out all the uncleanness that they found in the temple of the Lord into the court of the house of the Lord. And the Levites took it, to carry it out abroad to the brook Kidron."* After finishing the task, the priests reported back to Hezekiah and told him that the work was done and the temple was cleansed. The priests had even repaired and sanctified the vessels and temple tools that had been used previously. Hezekiah immediately had them to begin the sacrifices unto the Lord. Of course, we know that the salt began to be poured out again in Israel for every sacrifice had to have salt on it. (See Lev. 2:13)

Hezekiah the king got together with the priests, and they renewed their salt sacrifices unto the Lord. They entered into a covenant with Him, and they had a revival. There it is again, the priest and the king. The pattern is clear. The king and the priest work as one. When you see this, you see Melchisedec. You see Jesus the Messiah, who is King of kings and the great High Priest. Jesus, King and Priest, said He is the bread, or the sacrifice, and we apply the salt of the covenant as new covenant priests under the High Priest.

> ## *The joy of the Lord*
> ## *was restored to Israel.*

Hezekiah went on to institute all of the offerings and the blood sacrifices. He reinstated the families of the priests who were worshippers, singers and musicians to the offices that David had appointed them. They began to sacrifice the burnt offerings to the Lord again. In 2 Chronicles 29:35 it says, *"So the service of the house of the Lord was set in order."* Then in verse 36, *"And Hezekiah rejoiced, and all the people."* The joy of the Lord was back in the land. The move of God intensified. It was a glorious move of the Lord.

Hezekiah went on to reinstate the Passover feast. There was a tremendous intolerance for idolatry that arose as the revival continued. They broke in pieces all of the idols and tore down the altars of pagan worship. The people all agreed that there had not been a move of God like this since the days of Solomon the king (2 Chronicles 30:26). It all started by the correcting of the priesthood and the corporate anointing of the king and the priest. Again, it is God's pattern. The priests have to be walking in the covenant of the Lord. This was clearly understood by all the kings of Israel. Hezekiah had a heart to seek the Lord and enter into the covenant, so the first thing he did was call the priests together and lead them into sanctification and personal holiness. That is a type of the salt of the covenant. Hezekiah didn't start by building a great army or an arsenal of weaponry. He started right where he had to start, with the priesthood.

> ### *God is a God of pattern.*
> ### *He never changes.*

When I first began to see this pattern in the Bible, my heart was so touched. I realized that we are the priesthood under the new covenant, and that the Lord will deal first with His priesthood. We have to carry forth the filth out of the holy place, not to become priests, but because we are priests. Then, we must begin to offer again the sacrifice with salt on it. All of these powerful truths and the revelation of the covenant of salt made me see just how important the salt covenant is going to become in the last day. Once you see it, you see it all through the Bible. The Lord's problem is not with the heathens or the infidels, but with His priesthood. He will correct the priesthood prior to a great move of God.

We can see this same pattern plainly in the days of King Solomon. The chief priesthood in the early days of King Solomon was divided in that there were two men in that office, Abiathar and Zadok. Both of these priests had served Solomon's father, King David, and had shared the prestigious office of the chief priest. Thirteen times in the Scriptures we find them mentioned in the same verse. Zadok and Abiathar worked together. They marched before the ark together, and they served King David side by side. At a single glance it looks as if the two were equal in service and equal in their credibility. However, when Solomon was installed as king after the death of his father David, one of the first things he did was to get rid of Abiathar. It is recorded in 1 Kings 2:35, *"And Zadok the priest did the king put in the room of Abiathar."* Abiathar could have been judged for his disloyal behavior during the rebellion of Absolom against David, and I believe that was a factor, but there was much more than that. There is Bible proof that Abiathar was not in the covenant. In addition to not being in the covenant, he was under a curse. Abiathar was under a curse by a prophetic utterance spoken in the days of Eli, at a time of an earlier correcting of the priesthood. Don't forget the pattern. Before the Lord moves, He corrects the priesthood by bringing His priests into the salt covenant.

WALKING IN THE COVENANT OF SALT

Eli was a fat, soft on sin, compromising priest, without salt or personal holiness. He had allowed his sons to corrupt the priesthood and had placed their comfort above God's commandments. The Lord sent a special prophet to rebuke Eli, and to pronounce the judgment of the Lord against him. The Bible doesn't give us the name of the prophet, but we read the prophecy in 1 Samuel 2:27-33: *"And there came a man of God unto Eli, and said unto him, Thus saith the Lord, Did I plainly appear unto the house of thy father, when they were in Egypt in Pharaoh's house? And did I choose him out of all of the tribes of Israel to be my priest, to offer upon mine altar, to burn incense, to wear an ephod before me? and did I give unto the house of thy father all the offerings made by fire of the children of Israel? (Numbers 18:19 confirms that this was given by a covenant of salt.) Wherefore kick ye at my sacrifice and at mine offering, which I have commanded in my habitation; and honourest thy sons above me, to make yourselves fat with the chiefest of all the offerings of Israel my people? Wherefore the Lord God of Israel saith, I said indeed that thy house, and the house of thy father, should walk before me for ever: but now the Lord saith, Be it far from me; for them that honour me I will honour, and they that despise me shall be lightly esteemed. Behold, the days come, that I will cut off thine arm, and the arm of thy father's house, that there shall not be an old man in thine house. And thou shalt see an enemy in my habitation, in all the wealth which God shall give Israel: and there shall not be an old man in thy house for ever. And the man of thine, whom I shall not cut off from mine altar, shall be to consume thine eyes, and to grieve thine heart: and all the increase of thine house shall die in the flower of their age. And this shall be a sign unto thee, that shall come upon thy two sons, on Hophni and*

Phinehas; in one day they shall die both of them. And I will raise me up a faithful priest, that shall do according to that which is in mine heart and in my mind: and I will build him a sure house; and he shall walk before mine anointed for ever."

God's judgment falls on the corrupt priesthood.

Notice the severity of the judgment of the Lord on the corrupt priesthood. Eli's posterity is going to be cut off, except for one man. That one man will still serve the altar of the Lord, but only to continue to bring shame to the house of Eli. Samuel and his seed is the faithful priesthood that will do the will of the Lord and correct the priesthood. This particular faithful priesthood will be installed perpetually and walk before the Anointed One or the Messiah. This was a very powerful prophecy, covering great spans of time, with accuracy that can only come from the Lord. This unknown prophet spoke the Word of the Lord.

Years after this prophecy, Saul was anointed king of Israel, but David was being raised up to correct the kingship. Saul, out of jealousy, was trying to kill David. While fleeing from Saul, David went down to Ahimelech the priest in the city of Nob. David was without a weapon, and his men were without supplies. David told Ahimelech the priest that he was on business for the king and needed a weapon and some victuals. Ahimelech gave him the sword of Goliath and the shewbread off of the altar, and David went his way. There was a certain Edomite named Doeg who witnessed this transaction. When Saul got to Ahimelech, Doeg told Saul the whole story. Saul accused Ahimelech of treason. He went into a rage and commanded that the entire priesthood be wiped out, then went on to destroy the city. All of these were the descendants of Eli. Just as the man of God had prophesied, only one man of Eli escaped, and that was Abiathar. Fearing for his life, he ran to the camp of David and reported to him all that had happened at Nob by the hand of Saul. David's response is recorded in 1 Samuel 22:22-23: *"And David said unto Abiathar, I knew it that day, when Doeg the Edomite was there, that he would surely tell Saul: I have occasioned the death of all the persons of thy father's house. Abide thou with me, fear not: for he that seeketh my life seeketh thy life: but with me thou shalt be in safeguard."* David was unaware of the prophetic curse on Abiathar and was, no doubt, operating out of guilt. He was making an effort to make somewhat of a restitution to Abiathar; nevertheless, Abiathar was installed into the office of the priest for the wrong reason. According to the pattern and prerequisite concerning the priesthood, Abiathar had to go before the glory of the Lord would fall on Israel. God is a God of pattern.

The Lord is really not unpredictable.

A preacher was pouring out his complaint to me one day by saying, "I can never figure the Lord out. He is so unpredictable. He never does anything the same." I told him, "I find just the opposite to be true. He is a God of pattern, and therefore He is more than predictable." Maybe we can't always understand why we face this or that. We may not understand the manifestations of the Holy Spirit at times. But one thing we can count on is that the Lord Jesus is always the same, and He will never vary from Bible pattern. It is very evident through a study of the Scriptures, from one end of the Bible to the other; the Lord has set the standard for His outpouring. Before the glory falls, the pattern has to be right.

We can see how particular the Lord is in the matter of Abiathar and Zadok. The Lord has a special plan for the Zadok priesthood. This is the faithful priest that the Lord promised to raise up who would walk before His Anointed forever. David knew the difference between Zadok and Abiathar, and no doubt he was aware of a problem with the priesthood. He may have told Solomon, or perhaps it was the supernatural wisdom of the Lord that caused Solomon to put out Abiathar and establish Zadok. Whether or not David knew what the problem was, the fact remains that it had to be corrected before the fire fell. After the priesthood was corrected, the glory of the Lord fell on Israel like it never had before. That is why the Jews today who study the Torah look and long for the Zadok priesthood. The prophet Ezekiel said the Lord is going to use the Zadok priesthood during the millennium for His special priesthood. We find this confirmed in Ezekiel 44:15 and 48:11. The Lord says in both verses that only the sons of Zadok of the Levites can come close to the altar because they were faithful to Him. Zadok has the correct Aaronic bloodlines. He is the priest who walked in covenant with the Lord, and it is the sons of Zadok who will walk before the Anointed of the Lord during the millennium.

It is amazing to me that this pattern is so clearly seen through the verses, yet so completely ignored by many so called revivalists. Every time in the Scripture you see the king and the priest together in covenant before the Lord, you will see the glory of the Lord displayed.

I mentioned that during the dynasty of King David, the priesthood was incorrect. Abiathar was in office and had not yet been removed. Even during those days, we can see how the king and the corrected priesthood got together as the glory of the Lord was displayed. When King David was moving the precious Ark of the Covenant from the house of Obededom, he did something very controversial. He put on a linen ephod and danced before the Lord. The beloved Ark of the Covenant was finally coming home after a first attempt to return it had failed. The desire of David's heart was to build a resting place for the Ark. We understand from reading Psalm 132:3-5 that nothing was as important to David as erecting that house for the Ark of the Covenant and bringing it to Jerusalem. He said, *"Surely I will not come into the tabernacle of my house, nor go up into my bed; I will not give sleep to mine eyes, or slumber to mine eyelids, Until I find out a place for the Lord, an habitation for the mighty God of Jacob."* David was finally seeing his desire, and as they were bringing the Ark home, David put on a linen ephod and danced before the Lord with all his heart. He was actually wearing the attire of the Levites, even though he was of the tribe of Judah.

> ## *David personified*
> ## *the King and Priest together in Covenant.*

This is not the first time David acted as a priest. For some reason David could do this and Saul could not. When Saul tried to offer a sacrifice, he was strongly rebuked by Samuel. Yet David offered a sacrifice and the fire of the Lord fell. Then, he danced before the Ark of the Covenant while wearing a linen ephod, which was worn only by the priests. We see this as the king and the priest coming together at this very important moment in history through one man, David. In David's loins was the One to come who is the King of kings and the great High Priest. David by-passed the corrupt priesthood of his day to go on, in type, to the priesthood after the order of Melchisedec.

I believe that David, whom God used to utter many Messianic prophecies, could see in the spirit something almost like what we call Palm Sunday. David could see prophetically the Messiah coming to Jerusalem as king and priest. He could see the Ark in human form coming to Jerusalem, and the spontaneous worship and praise coming from the people in a glorious and splendid entrance to the city called Zion. That, I believe, is why David could wear the priestly garment. The priesthood must be corrected. The king and the priest must be united in holy covenant. That is when the glory falls.

The new covenant royal priesthood of believers, walking in the covenant of salt, will see the glory fall. God will have a Zadok remnant that walks before His anointed in holiness. They will do exploits because they know their God. Everything will be in beautiful divine order.

CHAPTER SIX

FOUR WAVES OF REVIVAL
AND THE SALT COVENANT

The covenant of salt cannot be removed from a real revival, and a real revival cannot be removed from the salt covenant. They are like prayer and fasting. You can't separate them. When people embrace the covenant of salt, there is going to be a revival. When you see a revival, you can always find the covenant of salt. There has never been a true revival that did not embrace personal holiness, neither has there ever been a great outpouring that wasn't preceded by preaching and teaching the blood of Jesus only for redemption. A close look at all the revivals in the Bible and those documented in history will reveal this truth.

There have been three major waves of revival that have swept the earth since the days of the Apostles. There have been several pockets of revivals or outpourings down through history, but there have been only three worldwide waves of revival. I firmly believe that a fourth wave of revival will encompass the world before the visible return of the Lord Jesus Christ. Praying saints around the world are saying the same thing. Intercessors from different countries are hearing the same thing from the same Spirit. The prophetic utterance of the coming revival is reaching a glorious crescendo.

> *Another worldwide revival*
> *is necessary to fulfill*
> *the latter rain pattern of the Bible.*

Let us examine the three past worldwide waves of revival in light of the covenant of salt. Then, I will attempt to validate the cry of the remnant church that insists it will see this last worldwide wave of glory. Many theologians agree that the true church of Jesus Christ will migrate back to Apostolic signs and wonders before the return of the Lord. As discussed previously, the church must go beyond that point in order to fit the pattern of the latter rain being more than the former rain. If a wave of revival of that magnitude is about to encompass the world, and I believe it is, then there must be signs of its appearing. I believe we will be able to see these signs if we study the past waves. We will also be able to identify the flavor and unction of this fourth wave by closely examining God's patterns.

First, we must readily admit that the Lord has had a remnant in every age. There has always been a group of people on earth who are enjoying revival in their hearts. You can have a personal revival, all by yourself, any time you line up with the Word of God and get in His divine pattern. When we speak in general terms of the church's condition or its aspirations, we must not forget that there are saints on earth who are already walking where the church needs to walk. There has never been a restraint on anyone who wants to get under the shadow of His wings. The Lord doesn't hold anyone back because of dispensation. He simply says, *"Draw nigh to me and I will draw nigh to you."* Anyone who really desires that, no matter what the rest of the world is doing, can achieve personal revival and go to great depths in the Spirit.

> *God wants His remnant walking in His divine pattern now.*

The Lord is no respecter of persons. Enoch went into the presence of the Lord, and just stayed there. You can't tell Brother Enoch that you can't get caught away yet because it is not time for the rapture. I say to hungry saints frequently, "Wait on no one to go in with you; move on past the inner court. He will meet you there." I think strict dispensational teachings often cause people to wait unnecessarily for things the Lord wants them to have now. Actually, the saints can now enjoy many of the same things that will earmark the millennium reign of Christ, even though the devil has certainly not been bound yet--unless he has a very long chain!

The waves of revival that have swept the world since the days of the Apostles were all in the dispensation of the church age; yet they each had a distinct flavor about them. The first wave was the Great Reformation, and the earmark was that of grace and pardon. The second was the Wesleyan revival, and its earmark was that of holiness and sanctification. The third wave was that of Pentecostal manifestations and gifts, starting for the most part in Wales, then spreading to America and the rest of the world. Its flavor was that of spiritual gifts and empowerment to the believer by the baptism of the Holy

Ghost and fire.

Martin Luther was mightily used in the first worldwide wave, and he certainly practiced holy living. In fact, he used his holy living to try to find favor with the Lord. Luther also saw some spiritual gifts and manifestations. However, the main ingredient in the Reformation revival was that of grace alone for salvation. Whitefield, Wesley, the Moravians, and others who were instrumental in the great Wesleyan revival certainly understood salvation by grace, or justification. They, too, saw some manifestations and operational gifts of the Spirit at work, but the theme or flavor of the Wesleyan revival was that of personal righteousness, or sanctification.

The Wales revival moved to America and New Zealand. The people who were used of God in this wave certainly knew the grace of God. Roberts, Bartleman, Seymour, and others were walking in personal righteousness, but the unction of this move was the baptism of empowerment by the Holy Spirit, producing gifts and manifestations. I sincerely believe that the fourth wave will embrace all of the attributes of the first three waves. I believe that the flavor of this fourth worldwide wave will be that of the revelation of the deity of Christ and intimacy with Him. I am not implying that Martin Luther or John Wesley did not enjoy the revelation of the deity of Christ or intimacy with Him, but I believe that the coming revival will be earmarked by these attributes.

> *The four worldwide waves of revival*
> *are in harmony with the four gospels.*

The four Gospels, Matthew, Mark, Luke and John each had a different theme, though the writers all enjoyed the same things. Matthew was a recipient of His grace. He answered the call to separation from the world. He was in the upper room and experienced the gifts and empowerment of the Holy Ghost, but his Gospel portrays Jesus as the King. Mark's Gospel portrays Christ as a servant. Luke portrays Him as a man. The Gospel of John portrays Him as God almighty in the flesh. Each Gospel has a flavor that is different from the others.

Many Bible scholars believe that the four headed beast in the book of the Revelation is representative of the four Gospels because each head represents a theme of each of the Gospels. The Lion is a type of the king, as Matthew portrays Jesus. The ox is a type of the servant, as in the Gospel of Mark. The man represents Luke's portrayal of Jesus. The eagle is a type of loftiness or deity which is portrayed by the Gospel of John.

It is very interesting to me that each one of the worldwide waves of revival thus far follows the same pattern or theme as one of the Gospels. The first wave was that of pardon, and only the King can pardon. The second wave was that of holiness, which is an expression of gratitude and servitude by a pardoned soul. The third wave was that of empowerment by the Spirit, which is needed by this pardoned servant, because he is just human. The fourth wave will lift the church to that lofty level only attained by people who have been pardoned and empowered, who are living holy as an expression of servitude, and walking intimately with Christ in the revelation of His deity. It will be a "John's Gospel" revival. It will be a latter rain outpouring that will certainly be greater than the former. This revival will be a move of God that causes believers to see Jesus as God Almighty in the flesh. They will enter into a deep, intimate relationship with Him. This is definitely John. He knew the pre-existence of Jesus and His deity; yet, he leaned on His breast.

> *The fourth wave of worldwide revival*
> *will sweep the world*
> *with the revelation of the deity of Christ.*

John's Gospel begins with these wonderful words full of the revelation of His deity: *"In the beginning was the Word, and the Word was with God, and the Word was God. The same was in the beginning with God. All things were made by Him; and without Him was not anything made that was made."* John saw Him as the pre-existent, eternal God who created the universe, manifesting Himself in a human body. John went on to confirm the revelation of Him as the Creator in John 1:10: *"He was in the world, and the world was made by Him, and the world knew Him not."* His own people didn't know that He was the Word made flesh. They couldn't see his deity. That is why they rejected Him.

John knew that Jesus was the Word made flesh. The early church knew He was God Almighty in the flesh. Hear the Apostle Paul in 1 Timothy 3:16, *"And without controversy great is the mystery of godliness: God was manifest in the flesh, justified in the Spirit, seen of angels, preached unto the Gentiles, believed on in the world, received up into glory."* Many Christians today have a very low view of Jesus, almost as if He is God the Second. This is very sad and unscriptural. The "John's Gospel" wave of revival that will sweep the world will cause people to see Him in His glory, as John did, with a full revelation of His deity. I believe this is beginning to take place now, and that it will intensify.

> ## *The prophets could see this church who knew their God intimately.*

Daniel records a group of elite saints who will do exploits in the end time because they know their God. (Daniel 11:32) Could his prophetic eyes have seen the end time New Covenant Priesthood, walking on this earth in an intimate relationship with Jesus, full of the revelation of His deity, trusting only His blood for redemption, living holy and separated from the world? Surely these are the ones who will do exploits and shake the world with the genuine power of God. This is the fullness of all the covenants of the Lord. This is the glorious church without spot or wrinkle that will torment every demon in hell until it is called out. The prophets of old could see this hour in the Spirit. They could see a group of glorious people on earth, walking in power, and causing the glory of the Lord to fill the whole earth. These people are most definitely the covenant people of the Lord. The salt covenant has everything to do with this final wave of revival.

Many times when I minister on the coming wave of glory, people get confused because they understand the Bible predicts a great falling away in the last days. Certainly the Bible does predict a coming apostasy. Verse after verse verifies that men will turn into mockers and scoffers of God. Everything holy and sacred will be despised by the apostates and the infidels. Demonic forces will launch an organized, orchestrated attack on everything that is holy. We already see it developing. However, the same Bible predicts a great outpouring of the Holy Ghost on believers in the last days.

There should be no confusion about this matter. What the Bible predicts will surely come to pass. The fact is that the outpouring of the Holy Ghost and the great falling away will come at the same time.

There is no question that the Lord will have a holy remnant who will overcome the wicked one. As things in the world get more evil, the remnant church will shine brighter. The devil is gathering his forces for the end time war. However, Jesus is moving among the seven golden candlesticks, and He is raising up a people who know their God intimately. They are being raised up to do exploits. The fact that evil seducers are waxing worse and worse (2 Timothy 3:13) substantiates the truth of a last day outpouring. I believe that these two moves will intensify at the same time. When sin and evil reach an all time high, God's true church will walk in more glory. The prophets could see it. They could see a remnant walking in the salt covenant that will enjoy this fourth worldwide wave of revival in the middle of the coming apostasy.

The Lord is pleading with the lukewarm church.

Revelation 3:16 describes three different possible conditions of a church. Actually, this verse may be describing three types of churches on earth at the time of the end. They are the hot church, the cold church, and the lukewarm church. The hot church represents the covenant people who embrace all of the covenants of the Lord, while trusting only His grace for salvation. The cold church is the apostate church or the false church on earth. The lukewarm church is the one that makes the Lord sick with grief, and the one that He is pleading with right now to come on over to the hot side. There is a holy call for the church to return to its first love. Those who answer that call will be a part of this final outpouring. This fourth wave will be the most awesome display of the Lord's power that the world has ever witnessed. It will come through His covenant people. It will be a culmination of all the other worldwide waves combined with this anointing of John's Gospel.

The salt covenant plays a significant part in this fourth wave of revival and can be seen clearly in the other worldwide waves of revival as well. Inspecting the former revivals in view of the salt covenant sheds much light on the coming fourth wave of glory. As we have established in the preceding chapters, salt, or shall we say good salt, is a type of personal holiness. This is not to be confused with imputed righteousness, which is the bread of the covenant.

Between 300 A.D. and 350 A.D. the church, for the most part, had lost its salt. Rome had made Christianity its state religion, and the true remnant church went underground. When the real church went underground, the world went into what is known as the Dark Ages. This was a horrible period of darkness and despair. The Roman church gained power and control during this time. Saints who received the revelation of salvation by grace apart from the Roman church were persecuted and often executed. Girolamo Savonarola was a monk who lived in the 1400's. He understood and preached the imputed righteousness of God and redemption by the blood alone. One of the accounts of his execution can be read in *Foxe's Book of Martyrs*. He was tormented daily until the day of his execution, but with a steadfast faith in Christ and the Word of God, he defied the Papal system. A Roman Cardinal read at his execution, "From the church militant and the church triumphant we do exclude you, O Savonarola." With great joy and victory in his voice, Savonarola replied, "From the church militant thou mayest exclude me, but from the church triumphant thou mayest never exclude me." As they hanged him and burned him alive, he sang and shouted.

> ## *The reformers*
> ## *were Salt Covenant people.*

Powerful, salty men and women such as this were the forerunners of the Great Reformation. Savonarola was already walking in strict personal righteousness before he discovered the matchless grace of the Lord and was born again. One minister heard me preaching on the salt covenant and said concerning saints like Savonarola, "They came into it backwards." It does appear so, but as discussed earlier, our salt without His bread is not good salt. Our righteousness is nothing but filthy rags. When we receive the bread of the covenant (Jesus said, *"I am the bread"*) then our personal righteousness becomes good salt. Personal righteousness, without the bread, is actually offensive to the Lord because people trust in their own righteousness to find favor with Him. The reformers did not quit living holy because they found the grace of God, any more than the Apostle Paul did. They were holy men of God who had learned to trust only the free gift of God's grace through the blood of Jesus for their salvation.

The movement gained power, and as time went on, the Great Reformation spread all over the world. Luther, Wycliffe, Hughes, Latimer, Knox, and a great host of others preached the Gospel of grace. These men lived holy and separated lives, but they did not trust in their holiness. They put salt on the bread. The revelation of God's amazing grace, or the bread, filled their souls with great joy. They learned that the personal righteousness they had was not their means of salvation but the result of it. Again, it was the great salt covenant at work. I love to read stories of the Great Reformation. I am inspired by the courage and the influence the saints had in that age. When you see that level of effectiveness, you can always find the covenant of salt.

With all the glory of that wave, there is still evidence that the reformers were not completely free from the Roman church, but the Reformation launched the church in the right direction. Each worldwide wave of glory has brought the church farther away from Rome and closer to the New Testament church standard.

> *The Wesleyan revival*
> *salted down England*
> *and spread around the world.*

The next wave, which began in the early 1700's, could be called the Wesleyan revival. Like the reformers, many of the mighty men used in this great revival came into the salt covenant in reverse. John Wesley, who founded the Holy Club of Oxford, was known for his pious discipline. By his own admission, he expected to attain God through his personal holiness. He practiced every imaginable form of self denial in order to please God. He would even sleep on the floor to buffet his flesh. He had such a pattern of pious living that the name Methodist was given to him and his followers. Wesley was very determined to make it to heaven as a servant of the Lord. Certainly his efforts were admirable, but they could not give him peace of mind or a witness in his spirit of genuine redemption. When he was finally converted at Aldersgate Street in London, England in 1738, he testified that his heart was strangely warmed by the power of the Lord. Wesley received the witness of the Holy Ghost that all of his sins were gone and he was a child of God. Wesley made a stirring statement in his diary later that week. He wrote, "I have tasted the bread of the sacrament many times and remained hungry, but now I have tasted the bread that came down from heaven, Jesus Himself.

The austere, disciplined life of Wesley, which before his conversion could never satisfy his aching heart, now caused him to be one of the most effective men for Christ who ever lived. He was now in the covenant of salt. He had received Jesus, the bread, and he already had the salt. Some historians claim that John Wesley affected the world as much or more than the Apostle Paul. Certainly he was the most effective man for Christ in his day.

Those holy Methodist ministers, trusting the blood of Jesus alone for their redemption, changed the world around them. These salt covenant people looked very different from so much of what we see today that is called Christian. John Wesley would never condone the carnality that is prevalent in many groups who claim to follow his teachings. The Wesleyan revival did lead the church farther away from Roman doctrine and back toward Apostolic faith and practice. The revival continued to gain momentum throughout the 1700's, and a great harvest of souls came into the Kingdom.

> ## *The ministers of the Wesleyan revival embraced the Salt Covenant.*

Francis Asbury was converted through Wesley's ministry and came to America with great zeal and courage. He followed Wesley's pattern and basically did in America what Wesley did in England. The fire of revival burned on into the 1800's with great strength. Wesley's death in the late 1700's didn't seem to slow it down at all. The persecution and hatred that the early Methodists encountered disappeared for the most part as the movement continued.

Another great preacher in those days was George Whitefield. He was a tremendously gifted orator. He was with John Wesley in the early days at Oxford. He was also aflame for Jesus and left behind him a host of genuine converts who helped to spread the fire even more.

It was on a cold, snowy night in England in the early 1800's that a young man entered into a little Methodist mission to warm himself, not knowing that his heart would also be warmed by the grace of God. His name was Charles Hadden Spurgeon. He later became known as the "Prince of Preachers." As a young man in his early 20's, his anointed preaching drew enough people to fill the 5000 seat Brooklyn Tabernacle twice each Sunday. He serves as an example of the far-reaching effects of the Wesleyan Revival. It was definitely a worldwide wave of glory.

This revival knew no social barriers. It had no favorite people or creed. General William Booth, founder of the great Salvation Army, was also saved as a result of this great revival. His firm belief that God could and would save anybody, his zeal for evangelism to the poor and needy, and his high standards of personal holiness made him a very effective force for the Kingdom of God. He was also a salt covenant preacher. Thousands of salty preachers of the gospel of grace came out of that movement. Actually, every evangelical group in the world today, when tracing its heritage back to the twelve Apostles, will come across this great movement.

Some writers of church history accredit the Anglican Church for this revival because John and Charles Wesley, as well as George Whitefield, were ordained ministers of the Church of England. It is true that John Wesley died an ordained minister of the Church of England. He never left his church, though more than once he was encouraged to do so. However, his conversion was directly connected to the ministry of the Moravians and a German minister, Peter Boehler, who made a covenant with 20 or 30 other Christians, to pray and seek God until the fire fell. They committed themselves to live absolute holy and separated lives before the Lord, and to call on the God of grace to move. Again, we see the great salt covenant at work. They did exactly what they covenanted to do, and God answered with fire. As a result, the Moravian Christians enjoyed a great harvest of souls in a short period of time. They sent out more missionaries in a 20 year period than the Church of England did in 200 years. As mentioned previously, it was a group of those missionaries who touched the life of John Wesley so tremendously in the ship on his return to England from America.

The Moravians were converts of the Protestant reformers. The true remnant church has moved from wave to wave of God's glory. That, too, is a Bible pattern. Whatever really belongs to the Lord is always being changed from glory to glory.

> ## *The third worldwide wave of glory had the attributes of the first two waves as well.*

Just as the Reformation inspired the Wesleyan revival, the Wesleyan revival inspired the third worldwide wave of revival that would take the remnant church closer to the loftiness of a John's Gospel movement. This third worldwide wave seems to have started in Wales and rapidly spread to several areas at one time. Reports from China, New Zealand, Wales, Australia, Africa, and America all seem to correspond with a turn of the century move of Pentecostal manifestations among hungry Christians.

In the first two waves of revival, there was not a lot of talk about the gifts of the Spirit or the baptism of empowerment. The term *sanctification* was often used in the great Wesleyan movement, but Wesley himself confessed that he understood little about the operational gifts of the Spirit. However, there was a great deal of manifestations around the Wesleyan movement. Falling on the ground under great conviction, groaning, and almost convulsion type behavior often occurred at the ending of Wesley's meetings. It was because of this that his diary often read after he preached in churches, "I was asked never to return." Wesley's critics often cited what they called "wild behavior" in condemning the early Methodists.

From the beginning, the third wave had more outward manifestations. In the Wales revival, it was often reported that people were out in the Spirit for days at a time, experiencing trances, dreams, visions and gifts of the Spirit. There is no indication that these people were seeking signs and wonders. The cry of Evans Roberts was simply, "Bend me." There was no doubt a lot of wildfire in this move as in any movement. But there were many genuine supernatural experiences that yielded great fruitfulness in Christ. There were reports from the Wales revival of powerful and uncommon manifestations, but the true fruit of the Spirit was being seen. Powerful, heart-wrenching intercession would come forth, often from little children and young adults. Cries of desperation from burdened souls were heard in this revival.

Evans Roberts, who was somewhat of a leader in the Wales revival, reports an uncommon experience in a letter to Frank Bartleman of California. Roberts wrote, "One Friday night last Spring, while praying by my bedside before retiring, I was taken up to a great expanse, without time or space. It was communion with God. Before this, I had a far off God. I was frightened that night, but never since. So great was my shivering that I rocked the bed, and my brother, being awakened, took hold of me, thinking I was ill." He went on to tell Brother Bartlemen that this occurred every night for three months, from 1:00 a.m. until 5:00 a.m. Some time after these experiences, Evans wrote his description of the depth of the move in South Wales. He wrote to the world, "The revival in South Wales is not of men, but of God. He has come very close to us." Because of His nearness they could sense His very heart to move across the world with His awesome glory.

> ## *A great awareness of God's desire to stir the world was prevalent.*

The revival in Wales had already started but had not yet spread to America when Frank Bartleman was stirred to write these words, "I believe that the world is upon the threshold of a great religious revival, and I pray daily that I may be allowed to help bring this about. Wonderful things have happened in Wales in a few weeks, but these are only a beginning. The world will be swept by His Spirit as by a rushing, mighty wind. Many who are now silent Christians will lead the movement. They will see a great light and will reflect it to thousands now in darkness. Thousands will do more than we have accomplished, as God gives them power." It was a prophetic word born out of intense prayer. Actually, this prophecy was written after a prayer meeting in Pasadena, California. Bartleman had a witness from the Lord that He was about to move mightily. Amos 3:7 tells us, *"Surely the Lord God will do nothing, but He revealeth His secret unto His servants the prophets."* The fire fell. The glory came. These were not sensationalists; they were intercessors. They were saints who allowed the Lord to bend their lives and get them in the salt covenant. Holy, separated prayer warriors arose from everywhere. The people prayed with a passion. Bartleman's recorded description of the depth of prayer tells the story: "Prayer was not formal in those days. It was God-breathed. It came upon us and overwhelmed us. We did not work it up. We were gripped with real soul travail by the Spirit that could no more be shaken off than could the birth pangs of a woman in travail, without doing absolute violence

119

to the Spirit of God. It was real intercession by the Holy Spirit."

Frank Bartleman kept in touch with Evans Roberts even after the fire fell at the Azuza Street Mission. The manifestations were not the real issue. It was the power of the Holy Ghost at work in the believers that wrought the work. Intercessors all over the world were testifying of a witness they had received that the revival would sweep the world.

The third wave sweeps the world.

In 1907, reports began to come that a modern day Pentecost had reached India. A mission in India by the name of Ramabai Mission gave the following report: "The girls (in the mission) were wonderfully wrought upon and baptized with the Spirit. Great light was given to them. When delivered, they jumped up and down for joy for hours without fatigue. In fact, they were stronger for it. They cried out with the burning that came into and upon them. Some fell as they saw a great light pass before them, while the fire of God burned the members of the body of sin, pride, anger, love of the world, selfishness, uncleanness, etc. They neither ate nor slept until the victory was won. Then the joy was so great that for two or three days after receiving the baptism of the Holy Spirit they did not care for food." What seemed to be consistent in this third worldwide wave of revival was that people who were blood washed were getting thoroughly right with God, and He was gloriously empowering them with a baptism of fire. Certainly the Lord would not entrust great power and manifestations to unholy vessels. The movement continued to grow and spread. A number of

Pentecostal denominations can trace their roots back to this turn of the century outpouring. Some of these denominations have millions of members. It has swept the world.

> ### *Get ready for the*
> ### *fourth worldwide wave.*

One hundred years later, intercessors are getting the witness again that we are on the verge of another worldwide wave of glory. The church has yet to reach the level of the early church, much less go beyond it. It will take an awesome move of God; but I firmly believe that it will happen, and that it is already beginning. The flavor of all the previous worldwide waves will be present, along with the fourth gospel, the Gospel of John. Of course, there are conditions and prerequisites for entering into the fourth wave. The glorious church the Bible talks about is ready to come forth and shine. All the things the prophets saw in the Old Testament concerning a holy priesthood walking on earth in power, doing exploits, will be manifested. Some are saying that the church is now in its finest hour. I believe such talk is a great hindrance to the remnant, and perhaps has caused some to be slack in prayer. The church is not in its finest hour. We are not in the last great revival yet. The spiritual ground is quaking and the bones of the thing are coming together. The prophets of our day are prophesying to the wind, but the exceeding great army has not yet stood.

> ### *The beginnings of the fourth wave*
> ### *are manifesting.*

Four Waves of Revival and the Salt Covenant

The Lord has had a remnant in every age that experienced His fullness. There are saints on earth today who are on the Holy Hill under the shadow of His wings, literally walking with Jesus in an intimate way. These are what I call real full gospel people. For many, the term *full gospel* means that the gifts of the Spirit are present, but that is only part gospel. Genuine moves of God are now stirring entire cities. There are praying saints who are shaking the heavens, but we are not there yet. I would not want to be the modern day prophet to announce to Isaiah or Daniel that this present church on earth is the one they saw in the Spirit. There must be another wave. There has to be another level of glory that the church will experience. There is no way that any honest Bible student could say that the church today is anywhere near where the Apostles were. Hearts are crying and melting with holy passion to see this manifest. It must come God's way, and He has chosen to move on men through the covenants. We must move in God's direction, not our direction, and certainly not the direction of organized religion.

Entering into real fullness requires adhering to God's pattern. There is no way around the covenants for entering into the fullness that must come. God's pattern is portrayed through the three previous waves of worldwide revival and will be completed by the fourth wave. Only those who are saved by grace are eligible to enter into true Bible holiness. This is the salt covenant, bread and salt. Only salt covenant people can be trusted with the true power of Pentecost. It is ridiculous for modern day Christians to think they will go from the bread to empowerment without any salt at all.

Leonard Ravenhill received much criticism when he drove power seekers from an altar, scolding them for wanting the power so they could feel good, instead of coming to the altar to die to self. The altar is a place of death. Christians who are dead to self are the ones the Lord can entrust with His mighty baptism of fire. Ravenhill's boldness actually came from a cry within his burdened soul. The cry is for no more shallow, saltless, unsanctified professors of Spirit fullness who are not possessors of the fullness. We must see that in order to go into the gifts and manifestations of the Holy Spirit, we have to be walking in the salt covenant. We can see the horrible devastation that has come from trying to enter into the gifts without the salt. This could be the reason the term *spirit filled* is one of the most misused Christian terms of our time.

> *The Salt Covenant people of the fourth wave will take the reproach away from Pentecost.*

We read in Ephesians 5:18, *"And be not drunk with wine, wherein is excess; but be filled with the Spirit."* We can see from this comparison that the Bible is really talking about being controlled by the Spirit. We are not to let wine control us, but we are supposed to let the Holy Spirit control us. I don't hear many Christians talk about being Spirit controlled. Many will say, "I'm Spirit filled," but few will say, "I'm Spirit controlled." The Bible uses the term *filled with the Spirit*, but it definitely means to be *controlled by the Spirit*. Yet it seems too much to say what it means. The reason it is easier to say Spirit filled is not just because it is a scriptural term. It is because the term has become a cliché among Christians to describe a group of people instead of a Biblical description of a holy, separated, Christ controlled life. People whose walk can not afford them to say they are controlled by the Spirit will often say that they are Spirit filled. Can you imagine professing Christians who are controlled by habits, lusts, and vile affections saying that they are Spirit controlled? Walking in the salt covenant by the power of the Holy Ghost shows the world a fill that is real. When this powerful, spirit-controlled covenant people operate in the gifts of the Holy Ghost, it will stop the mouths of the enemies of God. The religious people who tried to speak out against the first Pentecost were hushed by the display of the gifts of the Spirit. We see this in Acts 4:13-14: *"Now when they saw the boldness of Peter and John, and perceived that they were unlearned and ignorant men, they marvelled; and they took knowledge of them, that they had been with Jesus. And beholding the man which was healed standing with them, they could say nothing against it."* These holy, separated, and Spirit controlled men, operating through the gifts of faith and miracles, silenced the scoffers and brought glory to the name of Jesus. The wonderful gifts of the Holy Ghost are real, and they are certainly for our day, but there must be the salt of personal holiness involved. You cannot bypass holiness.

Leaning on His breast with full revelation

The third worldwide wave of glory did not come through unsanctified people who loved the world. Saints who were trusting the blood of Jesus for favor with God, and who walked in personal holiness, were baptized with the fire of Pentecost. Gifts and manifestations followed them, and this wave went around the world. The fourth wave will add one more dimension to the church's quest for the latter rain. This dimension is intimacy with Jesus in the full revelation of His deity. This is what the prophets saw. His glory will then fill the whole earth.

I firmly believe that we are now entering into the beginning of this great revival. The power and far reaching effects of this fourth wave will never be halted by the spirit of the antichrist, nor by his appearing, for that matter. Many will be given a martyr's crown. Many will be hated for the name of Jesus. But the church triumphant will march on, and the Gospel will be preached all over the world. This glorious remnant church will be viciously hated by the world's religions. The more she shines, the more she is hated. It has always been that way. The more glory the church has, the more she is hated by the world, the devil, and religion. The persecution will only add fuel to the fire. This remnant will do exploits because they know they are redeemed by the blood of the Lamb. They have given their bodies to the Lord as a living sacrifice and are walking in the salt covenant. They are empowered by the Holy Ghost and operating in the gifts of the Spirit, with signs and wonders. They intimately know the Lord Jesus. They are leaning on His breast, with a full revelation that He is God Almighty, the First and the Last.

CHAPTER SEVEN

THE CRY FOR SALT

Job asks a good question in Job 6:6, *"Can that which is unsavoury be eaten without salt? or is there any taste in the white of an egg?"* The reason for the cry for salt among the remnant church intercessors right now is because they can hardly eat the egg white Christianity of our generation. Lack of taste due to a lack of salt causes a cry and a hunger among the saints who are after the heart of the Lord.

There is a certain devastation that occurs when the church tries to go forward in its mission without salt. We have seen that devastation firsthand in what some call the neo-Pentecostal movement. Others call it the Charismatic movement, which began in the late 1960's and early 70's. A general lack of salt was and is prevalent. It claims all the power of the revival at the turn of the century, which we have classified as the third worldwide wave, but it looks and acts nothing like it. The message is so different. For the most part, it is not nearly as broken. The truly contrite heart and genuine repentance, followed by separation from the world seems hard to find.

There was no glamour around the Wales revival. There was no merchandising or marketing, just a clear exaltation of the Lord Jesus, coupled with a cry of repentance that groaned, "Bend me." In the beginning of that wave, there was salt. There was salt in the Wesleyan revival. There was salt in the Great Reformation, but where is the salt today? This is a great indication to the remnant that we are not yet in the fourth worldwide wave of revival. As mentioned previously, I believe we are seeing the beginning of it, or at least the preparation for it. Intercessors today who know the wind of the Spirit are crying for salt. It is settled in their souls that a genuine move of God has to be within the boundaries of God's covenants. Jesus made it very plain that every sacrifice must have salt on it. (See Mark 9:49) There will be no mighty move of God without salt.

> ## *The remnant is looking for the salt.*

Not long ago, a widely recognized leading authority in the field of church growth and spiritual warfare, wrote a book about the church's present condition. Certainly the book has a great amount of good solid Biblical information and is worthy to read; however, he almost scolds the church today for looking back to John Wesley, Charles Finney, Evans Roberts, Jonathan Edwards and others. I can see how always looking in the past could hinder intercessors for the present. I understand that we can't live on yesterday's blessings and spiritual outpourings. However, I also understand why some are looking back. We are looking back because we lost something back there. There was something we didn't bring with us in our journey to the last worldwide wave of glory. It is something we must have if we are to change the world. It is salt. Please don't scold us for looking back for the thing that is missing. We are not nostalgic. There can be no genuine "New Apostolic Reformation" without the salt of personal holiness, placed by the New Testament priesthood on the bread of imputed holiness, imparted to us as a gift of grace by the precious blood of Jesus. There never has been and there never will be a real revival, move, or reformation, without salt. That is why the body of true remnant believers is crying for salt.

Intercessors are crying for the salty ministers and laymen we read about in those past waves. Nobody has to inform the praying saints of this generation to cry out for salt. Saints who have never heard of the covenant of salt are crying for integrity to return to the body of Christ. We can see the physical parallel and understand why the Lord called for salt on the sacrifice. He could have called for a lot of different things to be put on the sacrifices of the Old Testament. Jesus didn't say, "Ye are the *sugar* of the earth." He used salt and quoted the Old Testament verse in Leviticus 2:13 about salt being on every offering. We can make it without sugar, but we must have salt.

> ### *The deep cry of the Spirit in man is for salt.*

There is a cry for salt that is as real in the spirit realm as the cry for salt in the physical realm. The human body has to have salt to function properly. It is not just to make our food taste better. Actually, in order to live, we have to have salt. I grew up on a farm in rural Kentucky and learned how important salt was for the livestock. I remember one particular scene that I have often thought of in connection with the salt covenant. My daddy and I went to the back side of our farm to check on the cattle and to put out salt for them. When my daddy called them, they were really excited and came bawling and running all the way to where we were standing. I asked my daddy why the unusual behavior from the cattle, and he told me that he was later than usual in getting the salt to the cattle. He said, "They know I have salt with me." He went on to explain to me how the cattle must have salt and how they crave it. This is a crude illustration, but it is certainly an accurate one concerning the church's cry for salt in our generation. No one has to tell us to crave salt. It comes naturally. We crave it because our body needs it. It is the same way in the spiritual realm. We crave salt because we have to have it. The body of Christ needs it. Even those who are struggling with walking in personal righteousness (salt) crave it.

I received a note from a fellow minister that read simply, "I am dying from a lack of salt, and the death on me is spreading fast." He had read the tract I wrote about the covenant of salt, and his heart was crying for good salt to go on the sacrifice. There are many Christians in this generation who are dying for salt, and they are looking for someone to supply it for them. Jesus said, *"Ye are the salt..."* in Matthew 5:13. In Mark 9:50, Jesus said, *"Have salt in yourselves..."* No one else can supply the salt for you. One of our fellow workers laid a note on my desk that read, "Pastor, please help me to discipline my life." That is an example of the cry in the body for salt. There is a cry for integrity, decency, honor, discipline, character, honesty, separation from the world, sanctification, consecration, fidelity, holy zeal, virtue, prudence, promptness, respectability, fervency, and old-fashioned righteous living.

> ## *We can't eat it without salt.*

I have read the famous sermon by Dr. Bob Jones, founder of the Bob Jones University, entitled, "Do Right." It is a masterpiece and worthy of any Christian's attention. It is said that Dr. Bob preached this sermon every year at the opening chapel service at Bob Jones University. One of the statements in the sermon is "Do right if the sky falls." People are sick of egg white ministry. They want to taste something savory. It is amazing to me, but people who aren't even walking in personal righteousness want to hear the truth. They hate it, but they are drawn to it. Even sinners do not respect a carnal, compromising, light, entertaining message from a minister who has no salt.

A modernist preacher went to the trouble to write an article in defense of social drinking among professing Christians. Perhaps he was trying to ease the guilt of himself and others. He even used the Scripture to try to prove that Christians can drink liquor. I was telling a man who had been an alcoholic before his conversion about the article. I love his response. He said, "I knew it was wrong to drink before I got saved. Now some preacher is trying to tell me it's all right?" Sipping saints may read an article like that to try to ease their conscience, but it won't work. Deep down, there is that cry for salt. Deep down, they know it is wrong. Homosexuals have worked very hard to get us to accept their perverted lifestyle as alternate. I am sorry to say it is working. The governing powers of some entire denominations have accepted their defense of this perversion. Perverts are coming out of the closet and sitting on the church pews, trying to show the world that they are all right just like they are. Regardless of how many members of society and undiscerning Christians are persuaded to accept them, the cloud of guilt and shame is still there. They know it is a sin before God. Every converted homosexual whose testimony I have heard or read verifies this.

Herod knew very well that he was not supposed to have his brother's wife. John, the salt preacher, told him it was wrong. It angered Herod and his new wife, but Herod knew he had heard the truth. He never got away from the words of John the Baptist. When Jesus started doing miracles, Herod thought He was John the Baptist raised from the dead. Herod probably thought he was going to have to look into those righteous eyes again. It is evident that Herod respected and feared John the Baptist. He didn't repent, as far as we know, but he heard the truth and respected John for preaching it. There was something about his holy man of God that caused Herod to tremble. Herod was aware of John's powerful influence on Israel. Those piercing eyes had no doubt unsettled the king.

> ## *Salt also irritates.*

It is said that the atheist in New York who opposed and hated Charles G. Finney, made one final request for his funeral. He said, "Don't let Charles G. Finney look at my corpse." No doubt, those piercing eyes had caused this man to suffer much. If the nineteenth century had any salt preachers, Charles G. Finney was one of them. People will listen to truth with salt on it. They may not always like it, but they will never forget it. They cry for it.

The world hates a compromising message. We see this illustrated perfectly in I Kings 22, an account of a war in the days when Ahab was king of Israel and Jehoshaphat was king of Judah. Ahab was not walking with the Lord. He had hired four hundred false prophets to tell him exactly what he wanted to hear. They were just hirelings, pulpit preachers who preached for money. They were ticklers of the ear. Isaiah called them dumb dogs that can't bark. I believe that Ahab despised these prophets because he could buy them. He knew they had no salt in their lives and knew that they would say whatever he wanted to hear. There was one prophet in that day that wasn't for sale. His name was Micaiah. When Ahab asked Jehoshaphat to help him in a military conflict with the Syrians at Ramoth-gilead, Jehoshaphat quickly agreed to help him. Then Ahab allowed his hireling prophets to prophesy in front of Jehoshaphat as we read in I Kings 22:6, *"Then the king of Israel gathered the prophets together, about four hundred men, and said unto them, Shall I go against Ramoth-gilead to battle, or shall I forbear? And they said, Go up; for the Lord shall deliver it into the hand of the king."*

> ## Jehoshaphat was crying for salt.

Jehoshaphat evidently either got a check in his spirit as these false prophets were prophesying, or he already knew they were performers for King Ahab. Jehoshaphat responded in verse 7, *"And Jehoshaphat said, Is there not here a*

prophet of the Lord besides, that we might enquire of him?"
Jehoshaphat is saying, "I want to hear from a true prophet.
I don't want to listen to four hundred egg white preachers."
Somehow in this I hear the cry for salt. Ahab knows exactly
what Jehoshaphat is looking for and he knows exactly who
will fit the bill. He answers Jehoshaphat in verse 8, *"And
the king of Israel said unto Jehoshaphat, There is yet one
man, Micaiah the son of Imlah, by whom we may inquire of
the LORD: but I hate him; for he doth not prophesy good
concerning me, but evil. And Jehoshaphat said, Let not the
king say so."* Micaiah had the testimony of being an "other."
At Jehoshaphat's request, Ahab sent someone to get Micaiah
the prophet.

While the messenger was getting Micaiah, the salt
covenant prophet, the false prophets intensified their act. One
of the phony prophets even used a skit to preach his message,
as we see in verses 11 and 12: *"And Zedekiah the son of
Chenaanah made him horns of iron: and he said, Thus saith
the LORD, With these shalt thou push the Syrians, until thou
have consumed them. And all the prophets prophesied so,
saying, Go up to Ramoth-gilead, and prosper: for the LORD
shall deliver it into the king's hand."* This is amazing. Look
at the energy the lying spirits utilize to get their message out.
Jehoshaphat watches and is no doubt anxious for the real
prophet of the Lord to get there.

Micaiah had plenty of salt.

Meanwhile, the messenger of the king who was sent to
get Micaiah finds him and tries to convince him to go along
with the other prophets. As we read in verse 13: *"And the*

messenger that was gone to call Micaiah spake unto him, saying, Behold now, the words of the prophets declare good unto the king with one mouth: let thy word, I pray thee, be like the word of one of them, and speak that which is good."

I believe all salt preachers have had an experience similar to this. They have been confronted with a request to compromise. They have encountered an effort from the world, the devil, the flesh, or perhaps organized religion, to deliver a word that will fit in with their message. Compromisers and hirelings are always trying to get the true man of God to change his message. If a man of God will compromise the truth, he doesn't have the salt. If he has the salt, he won't compromise the truth.

Micaiah had plenty of salt. He let this little pulpit committee know quickly that he wasn't for sale. We read his report in verse 14: *"And Micaiah said, As the LORD liveth, what the LORD saith unto me, that will I speak."* There would be many empty pulpits in America if every preacher had to be elevated to this lofty standard. There is a cry in this land for salty men of God like Micaiah. He stands before King Ahab and almost mocks the king, as we see in verse 15, *"So he came to the king. And the king said unto him, Micaiah, shall we go against Ramoth-gilead to battle, or shall we forbear? And he answered him, Go, and prosper: for the Lord shall deliver it into the hand of the king."* At first glance, it seems that Micaiah did compromise his message, but a closer look reveals that Micaiah is driving home the real message. I believe he is saying to the king by his answer, "You know full well that your prophets are phonies. You know that the real message of God is going to be exactly opposite from your hirelings. You know when I sound like them, I can't possibly be giving you the truth."

The king's response to Micaiah's taunting proves the powerful effect of Micaiah's tactics. Verse 16 says, *"And the king said unto him, How many times shall I adjure thee that thou tell me nothing but that which is true in the name of the LORD?"* At this point, Micaiah opens his mouth and lets the Lord fill it. Every eye in the place is upon him. Every ear is waiting for this one voice. The intercessors of this generation are praying for this very thing. They want all the hirelings to be put to silence and everyone to focus on the salt covenant preachers who are delivering the truth in righteousness. The Bible states in 1 Peter 2:15, *"For so is the will of God, that with well doing ye may put to silence the ignorance of foolish men."*

> ## *Truth, delivered through a vessel of honor will penetrate.*

Truth is not always received, but it carries great weight when distributed by a vessel of honor. The cry in this hour is for vessels of honor to preach the truth, and vessels of honor won't preach anything less. All of these false prophets either hated Micaiah or they were jealous of him, but they were all listening to him. Look at the respect he carries, even with his enemies. He definitely has the ear of all the people. Micaiah basically tells Ahab that he is going to be killed in the battle and that Israel will lose this campaign against the Syrians. He went on to scathe the false prophets by telling them they were operating under the influence of lying spirits. He told Ahab that he was being seduced by these lying spirits to go right into a battle that would cost him his life. After Micaiah's sermon, the chief false prophet responded with violence, as we read in verse 24: *"But Zedekiah the son of Chenaanah went near, and smote Micaiah on the cheek, and said, Which way went the spirit of the Lord from me to speak unto thee?"* This hired prophet is so angry that he slaps Micaiah and insinuates that the Spirit of the Lord could not speak to Micaiah unless it came through his office. The king also is angry and commands that Micaiah be put in prison and be given bread and water only, until he returns from the battle.

This, I believe, is nothing more than an effort to get Micaiah to alter his message. Micaiah had prophesied the king's death by the true word of the Lord. Between the lines, Ahab is saying to him, "If I don't return, you will die in that prison." Micaiah doesn't flinch. This preacher is a salt preacher. He is loyal to the Lord and His word. We read his response in verse 28: *"And Micaiah said, If thou return at all in peace, the LORD hath not spoken by me. And he said, Hearken, O people, every one of you."* No doubt, the words of the prophet tore at the king all night. Oh, the power of the truth in a vessel of honor!

King Ahab manifests his wholesale foolishness by making an effort to get around the prophecy delivered to him by Micaiah. The next day King Ahab changes his clothes before he goes out to the battle, thinking that no one will know that he is the king. Isn't it ridiculous to try to hide from the Word? Ahab didn't repent, but this is evidence that the truth was heard, and that he truly respected the man of God. Ahab went on to battle and, of course, he was killed just like the prophet had said. The record of his death is found in verses 34 and 35: *"And a certain man drew a bow at a venture, and smote the king of Israel between the joints of the harness: wherefore he said unto the driver of his chariot,*

Turn thine hand, and carry me out of the host; for I am wounded. And the battle increased that day: and the king was stayed up in his chariot against the Syrians, and died at even: and the blood ran out of the wound into the midst of the chariot."

King Ahab is forever an example of the destruction that comes to those who ignore the truth delivered through a vessel of honor. Micaiah is forever an example of an uncompromising man of God, dedicated to the truth of God's Holy Word, seasoned with the salt of personal holiness. The whole world is crying to see some Micaiahs.

Jehoshaphat, who is a type of careless Christianity, is hanging around outside the salt covenant, but he has enough discernment to know that something is wrong. He is crying for the salt. Jehoshaphat should never have made a league with wicked Ahab. Even Ahab knows the difference between his hireling phonies and the true man of God.

Something is missing.

Sometimes people will tell me that they enjoy certain preaching and Christian programming then they will follow this statement by saying, "There is just something missing." They are so right. There is something missing. They are like Jehosaphat. They are listening to all of this prophesying, but what they really want is to hear from Micaiah.

Among the youth there is intensity in the cry for salt. There is almost an anger among the Christian youth concerning the horrible lack of salt. The youth of this generation are appalled at the compromise in the pulpits. They are crying for salt. Egg whites don't taste good. They have no taste. The real shortage of our generation is a shortage of Christians with salt. When there is a shortage of something as dear as this, it produces a cry in the land. I hear it everywhere I go.

Some years ago, I had the privilege of preaching in and around Brisbane, Australia. I was there shortly after several famous preachers in America had fallen. You could sense the distrust in the air and almost see a manifested question mark on the foreheads of the people in the congregation. They were wondering if this was another American preacher who preaches one thing and does another. With the question mark, I could hear a cry for salt. I felt like they were saying, "Please don't let me find out that this preacher is not walking in holiness."

Church congregations are crying for salt in the pulpit. Declining membership in every mainline denomination except one can be easily interpreted as a cry for salt. Many of the leaders of these denominations thought it might be good for their growth if their message was more compatible with the world and modern times. They have proven to be so wrong! They, for the most part, have lost their salt; therefore, the world doesn't take them seriously. Their own members have trouble taking them seriously. Salt makes the difference.

The salt of John Bunyan

In the 1600's there was a holiness preacher by the name of John Bunyan who preached the gospel of grace. We know him as the author of Christianity's third all time best selling book, *The Pilgrim's Progress.* His life is so amazing and inspiring. What many people who read this book don't know is that the book was written in the Belford Jail. The Queen had issued an order that required all clergy to be licensed by the Parliament. John Bunyan firmly believed that to take the license would compromise the Lordship of Jesus over the ministry he had been called to do. He refused to take the license.

The other ministers who had taken the license came against John and reported him. They demanded that something be done to him. He was incarcerated several times, and for the most part of thirteen years, he was in the Belford Jail. John continued to preach every way he could through his writings. Tracts and books that are still being read today are the result of John Bunyan's wise use of the time he was incarcerated. During his lonely days in the Belford Jail, God gave John Bunyan one of the clearest and most powerful Christian allegories that the world has ever witnessed, *The Pilgrim's Progress*.

Many pleas were made by different parties for John to take the license and go free, but to no avail. They even approached his wife and tried to get her to persuade John to compromise his stand. The Bunyans had a child with a disability, and certainly John's prolonged incarceration had brought a lot of hardship on the family. The liberal persuaders thought to gain a foothold through what they considered to be the weaker vessel. When they pressed Mrs. Bunyan hard, she responded in a way that shocked her hecklers. She said, "I miss my John and we need him home very badly." She then paused and lifted up the apron she wore over her dress to fashion a sort of basin and said, "But I had rather have his head severed and laying in this apron than to see him compromise his stand for the Lordship of Jesus Christ over his ministry." That was their final conversation with Mrs.

John Bunyan on that matter. She salted them good. Part of the salt of personal holiness is uncompromising loyalty, which is horribly missing in our generation. There is a great cry for loyalty.

In the thirteenth year of John's imprisonment, his enemies pressed upon the Queen to execute John Bunyan and so rid the country of such a rebel. This also backfired on them, because the Queen released John Bunyan, saying that he had more faith and courage than all of the rest of the ministers put together. I call it salt. John could have easily taken the other route and spared himself a lot of hardship, but there was something beating in his breast that caused him to hate unholy compromise. He was willing to pay the price of consecration, for which Christianity shall ever be thankful. How have we missed this type of heart for truth and holiness? Where is the salt? I am crying to see it in the body again. No wonder some of us are looking back on the revivals of days gone by. We are looking for something called salt.

> *The wholesale compromise in churches is intensifying the cry for salt.*

A recent personal experience has really caused the cry for the salt of personal holiness and character to intensify in me. A young man who had been caught and charged with theft was brought to our ministry. He was rightfully facing serious charges for his crime. I agreed with the court to do his counseling and to provide housing for him through our ministry rather than have him incarcerated.

In the course of doing his counseling, I was shocked at what I discovered. My counseling is neouthetic, so we got right to the point in our first two sessions. I was going fairly fast and intense because the young man was raised in a "Full Gospel Church." I was going over basic fundamental teaching, which I assumed he had already heard. As I presented the Biblical standard of holiness and explained genuine repentance, I could tell I wasn't getting through to him. I stopped and said to the young man, "You're not getting this. Haven't you heard these things before?" I felt a righteous indignation rise up inside of me and before I knew it, I said, "What did you do in church all of your life?" I sat there totally amazed as this young man told me that his church had singing groups, concerts, trips to amusement parks, and all kinds of programs and events. What he described sounded like a spiritual social club that was void of salt.

I began to weep as I thought about the thousands of kids just like this one who grew up in neo-Pentecostal ministries that missed the message of true holiness. There was no indication that he had heard any salt teaching or preaching. In the church's zeal to keep the young people, it has compromised and competed with the world and has lost its salt. No wonder there is a cry for salt, even among our youth. As I sat there with this young man, I renewed my commitment to do everything in my power to properly challenge young people to live the deep walk of holiness and consecration. Egg whites won't feed them.

> ## *Compromise with the world produces saltless ministry.*

Many egg white ministries have used the world to try to reach the world and called it smart evangelism. They often quote the Apostle Paul in defense of their tactics, citing 1 Corinthians 9:20-22, *"And unto the Jews I became as a Jew, that I might gain the Jews; to them that are under the law, as under the law, that I might gain them that are under the law; To them that are without law, as without law, (being not without law to God, but under the law to Christ,) that I might gain them that are without law. To the weak became I as weak, that I might gain the weak: I am made all things to all men, that I might by all means save some."* How can any honest Bible student interpret this to justify compromise with the world? Should we dress up like a hard rocker, with smoke, lights and blaring guitars in order to reach kids hooked on music? God forbid!

Paul was certainly not a compromiser, and he did not preach or teach worldliness in any form or fashion. It was his pen that the Lord used to write to us, *"And have no fellowship with the unfruitful works of darkness, but rather reprove them."* (Ephesians 5:11) He rebuked Peter openly for compromising with the Jews. When he spoke of becoming one of them to win them, he was speaking of his heart for sinners and his intercession which allowed him to totally identify with them. Any step toward worldliness in order to win the world is a step down.

The dear Lord has called us out of this world and its ways. The Word says in 1 John 2:15-16: *"Love not the world, neither the things that are in the world. If any man love the world, the love of the Father is not in him. For all that is in the world, the lust of the flesh, and the lust of the eyes, and the pride of life, is not of the Father, but is of the world."* Billy Sunday said, "You can't really love flowers without hating weeds." Oh, how we need to walk in the great salt covenant as New Testament priests. Oh, how the world is crying for the salt of integrity in ministries.

The salt of Sam Jones

I have previously made mention of the great Methodist revivalist, Brother Sam Jones. The Lord used Sam Jones in a unique way. He was austere. He was very holy, and he had a tremendous intolerance for sin and compromise with the world. He also had a holy hatred for the liquor industry. Before he went to Nashville for a city wide crusade, he was threatened by a leading distillery owner and an owner of more than thirty riverboats by the name of Mr. Ryman. Mr. Ryman said, "If Sam Jones ever comes to this city, I'll run him out of town on a rail." Sam Jones went to Nashville. He got off the train, rented a carriage, and went straight to the Ryman mansion. He told the butler who answered the door that he was going to be the guest of Mr. Ryman, and then asked to be shown to his room. He also instructed the butler to call him for dinner.

At dinner, he was brought into the dining parlor and was seated right across from Mr. Ryman. Mr. Ryman was totally surprised and asked, "And who might this be?" Brother Sam Jones spoke up and said, "I'm Sam Jones, the man you were going to run out of town on a rail." After the initial shock of this statement, Mr. Ryman exclaimed, "Of all the audacity, to come into my home and sit at my table!" After a little stare down, he said to Sam Jones, "You might as well stay the night since you are already here." Sam Jones did stay that night, and the next night, and throughout his crusade. The media got wind of it, and thinking to cause a blemish on Brother Jones, reported that the evangelist for the city wide crusade was staying in the home of a well known miscreant. This had the opposite effect, and even more people came to hear Sam Jones preach. Mr. Ryman developed a love and admiration for the salty preacher.

During the second week of the crusade, Mr. Ryman began to attend the meetings. He was gloriously saved during that crusade. He sold his wicked business and later built a huge auditorium for Sam Jones to hold his meetings when he came to Nashville. It was called the Ryman Auditorium. This auditorium later became the home of the Grand Ole Opry, but it wasn't constructed for that purpose. It was built for the purpose of preaching the Gospel of Grace, and it was financed by a converted riverboat rogue to be used by a salt covenant preacher who stood for personal holiness and demanded it from those who named the name of Christ. We need to see more of that today. It is the salt that is missing in our city wide crusades. Even preachers who talk about personal holiness are light and entertaining. There really is a cry for salt in this land. Mr. Ryman saw it in the evangelist Sam Jones. May the Lord send some salty preachers like Sam Jones.

Some may know of the ministry of Sam Jones through the famous "Sam Jones Prayer Meeting" that took place in Winston-Salem, North Carolina during a city wide crusade. It seems that the clergy of the city who had called Sam Jones to preach the crusade were taken aback by his straightforward preaching and his scathing of sin in the pulpit as well as the pew. After a few nights of his "John the Baptist" type preaching, there arose a faction among the clergy to try to put a stop to Sam Jones' relentless attack on everything that is not perfect in the sight of God. They were afraid they would be hated by the entire community for calling Brother

Jones to be the evangelist in their city wide crusade. They didn't know how to go about this and appear Godly in their decision, so they called a prayer meeting.

Sam Jones was not aware of the meeting, of course, so he was out visiting and working the crusade. Ironically, but I believe by divine appointment, he came to the door of the house where several ministers were praying. At first he thought that was wonderful. He thought they were praying for the meeting and for the conversion of souls. He slipped into the room and knelt to pray along with them. He soon realized that the prayers were all about him. They were praying for the Lord to show them how to get rid of Sam Jones gracefully, how to save their credibility in the community, how to approach the organizers of the crusade about the matter, and a host of other things concerning the hot spot they considered themselves in.

When Sam Jones understood the situation, he remained silent until the last one was finished praying. Then, he lifted up his powerful voice and prayed, "Dear Lord in Heaven, please don't listen to a thing these preachers have asked you. Lord, you know if I change to be like them, I'll be as ineffective as these compromising cowards. Lord, please don't pay any attention to them." Needless to say, there was a lot of discomfort in the room as the embarrassed clergy tried to gain composure and respond. Sam Jones wisely requested that every faint-hearted soul withdraw from his connection with the crusade. He informed these ministers that there would be no compromise on his part. He called on them to take courage and stand with him for holiness and true repentance. He explained to them that the city was really crying for an uncompromising message, and that they would soon see a breakthrough. In a few days, that is exactly what they saw. Thousands were converted, and the city was never the same. Sam Jones could hear the cry for salt in that city.

> ## *There are no substitutes for salt.*

If there had been some preachers like Sam Jones instead of a compromising Lot in Sodom and Gomorrah, the cities would have been spared. There is absolutely no substitute for the salt of personal righteousness. The Lord allowed nothing else to season the sacrifices under the law. No leaven, no spice, no coloring, no liquid would suffice. They had to have salt.

There are no shortcuts to a real revival or real results in Christ. R.A. Torrey gave the prescription for revival in his discourse preceding his great crusade to Australia. He said, "If a few people, there need not be many, get thoroughly right with God and band together to seek the Lord, He will bring revival." This will work anywhere in the world with any people on earth. Though Torrey didn't use the term *salt covenant,* it is exactly what he was crying for and exactly what he knew would work. Being thoroughly right with God, of course, is receiving the bread of imputed righteousness. Putting the salt of personal holiness on that bread is the great salt covenant. Torrey went on to say that revival, or a visitation of God, is not so much a miracle as it is a result of lining up with God's standards. I heartily agree. It is so basic and simple.

> ## *My mother heard the cry for salt.*

THE CRY FOR SALT

I was converted at the age of nineteen in the basement of a little house in Leitchfield, Kentucky, where I lived with my sister and brother-in-law. That weekend, when I came home to my parents' house, I immediately told my mother that the Lord had come into my life and that I would never be the same again. We rejoiced together for a short time, and I told her that I was ready to do whatever the Lord Jesus wanted me to do. She then left my presence for a little while. When she came back, she had the address of a Bible verse written on a piece of paper. I never asked her, but I believe the Lord gave her that verse to give to me. It was Micah 6:8. She said, "This is what the Lord wants you to do."

I remember when I looked the verse up and the Holy Spirit burned my heart with these words, *"He hath shewed thee, O man, what is good; and what doth the LORD require of thee, but to do justly, and to love mercy, and to walk humbly with thy God?"* Even though the verse burned my heart, I really didn't see the power of it until years later when I began to preach the salt covenant. I see it now as a foundational verse and another of many references to the great salt covenant. The *"doing justly"* of Micah 6:8 is personal righteousness, and the mercy we are instructed to love is imputed righteousness.

I have certainly learned to love mercy. Only through the grace of God could I ever have any fellowship with the Lord Jesus. His wonderful grace and mercy have made me *"accepted in the beloved."* This is the bread, or the sacrifice, of the covenant. Through that grace, I have the power and anointing to do justly. This is personal holiness, which is the salt of the covenant. But it is only through Him. I must walk humbly before the Lord, offering the salt on the sacrifice, thus embracing the salt covenant. This is what the Lord wants, and this is what He ought to have. My mother was exactly right. The dear Lord had taught her the importance of loving mercy and doing right. This is the cry of the Spirit. Every city in the world is crying for the Christians to be the salt of the earth. Only those who are truly the blood washed disciples of Jesus and who walk in holiness and separation from the world can produce it.

Chapter Eight

The Salt of Consecration

Consecration is one of the dearest things to the heart of the Lord. To prove this, one of the most intriguing and moving services in the Bible is the Old Testament account of the ordination of Aaron and his sons with the ram of consecration found in Exodus, Chapter 29. Consecration was and is a massive portion of the Jewish religion. Messianic Jews have such lovely and meaningful worship services in the area of consecration. Consecration is deeper than sanctification, even though in some ways they are the same. Sanctification is the setting aside of someone or something for a holy use; consecration is the dedication of that which is sanctified. It is a glorious step beyond sanctification and holiness. Consecration is the sweetness and beauty of a surrendered life that is dedicated and devoted to Christ. Actually, consecration also has a connotation of perfecting that which is sanctified, or completing the sanctification.

THE SALT OF CONSECRATION

> ## *It is dangerous to fall short of consecration.*

It is imperative that sanctified individuals consecrate themselves completely to Christ. Without the work of holy consecration, the salt of personal holiness and the teaching thereof, can actually become a snare to the body of Christ. Neglecting or stopping short of consecration can negate even the salt that is resting on the bread of the covenant, which is imputed righteousness. There is a danger that salt covenant people who fall short of consecration will enter into horrible judgmental self-righteousness. This has been the shipwreck of many an advocate of Christian perfection or holiness. There is also the possibility that the unconsecrated proponents of the salt covenant will enter into a devastating and defeating war with the flesh by focusing on their own strength and ability.

We must see ourselves as a part of the New Covenant priesthood, embracing all of the covenant power of the Lord Himself. Then we can move into the wonderful realm of holy consecration. Once a believer sees the glory of resting wholly on the righteousness of the Lord, and living clean and holy for Him as a matter of consecration and devotion, the bondage of sin and self-struggle is over. The Lord wants us to be consecrated to Him, and He provides the dominion over the flesh and sin through weapons that are not carnal. This is why the salt covenant has everything to do with consecration, and consecration has everything to do with the salt covenant. God doesn't wink at sin, and because of that, He gives the sin hating Christian power over it. This power is released in the consecration of a New Covenant priest. The deepest commitment and service to the Lord Jesus is found in the sphere of consecration, after embracing the salt covenant.

> ## *The old hymns speak of holy consecration.*

The beloved saint and songwriter, Fanny Crosby, knew exactly what to cry out for in her desire to be drawn nearer to the precious side of Jesus. Though physically blind, she had great vision and insight into the deep things of God. The precious song, *"Draw Me Nearer"* came to her on a visit from her home in the busy city of New York to the beautiful home of Dr. William Howard Doane in Cincinnati, Ohio. While sitting on the porch in Ohio, watching a sunset through the eyes of the members of the Doane family, she had a deep realization that the creator of that beauty was the very one who bled and died to purchase her redemption. She indicated to the Doanes that she was receiving the words to a song and requested that they be written for her. She dictated it line by line, verse by verse, and then a chorus. Dr. Doane composed the musical score for it the next day, and a tremendous song was born that has stood the test of time. Every great tenet of the faith is found in the verses of that song—justification, sanctification, consecration, and our future glorification. The second verse deals beautifully with consecration. "Consecrate me now to thy service Lord by the power of grace divine. Let my soul look up with a steadfast hope and my will be lost in Thine." Consecration is sacred devotion and undying loyalty to the one who redeemed and sanctified us. It is a presenting of ourselves by dedication.

The wonderful ceremony of the consecration of Aaron and his sons recorded in Exodus is full of rich typology that enlightens us to the reality and need for Biblical consecration. Again, the covenant of salt has everything to do with consecration, as we will see in our inspection of that consecration service in Exodus 29. In this account of the ordination of Aaron and his sons, we find three different sacrifices. One is a sin offering, and the other two are burnt offerings. The sin offering is a bullock, and the burnt offerings are rams. Though the word *salt* is not mentioned in this chapter, we have clearly proven in the previous chapters of this book that the Bible is unwavering in its teaching that without salt there can be no sacrifice. It is emphatically taught in both the Old and New Testaments. (See Leviticus 2:13 and Mark 9:49) The Lord doesn't accept any sacrifice without salt on it.

Long after I began to teach and preach the covenant of salt, I realized that even though the Bible doesn't always mention it, there was always salt on the sacrifices. Through that knowledge, I have learned to think of salt when I think of sacrifice or offering.

> *There was salt*
> *on the ram of consecration.*

In Leviticus, Chapter 9, when Aaron offered the sacrifice that caused fire to come down, you can rest assured that he did not break the Bible standard of having salt on every sacrifice. The salt was there, even though it isn't mentioned. In 1 Chronicles, Chapter 1, did David offer the sacrifice that caused the fire to fall on Ornan's threshing floor without putting salt on it? No, he was very careful to follow every step of offering a sacrifice, especially this one, because it was offered to avert the plague that was on Israel. The salt was there, even though it is not recorded. When Solomon required the priests to offer sacrifices unto the Lord, then prayed the fire down, you can be confident the sacrifices were in divine order, and there was salt on them. The Bible doesn't record that salt was on the sacrifice at Mount Carmel, but you can rest assured that Elijah went by the Biblical Levitical order for the sacrifice. There was salt on Mount Carmel. The priest returning from exile with Ezra received an abundance of salt to take back with them to Jerusalem. The Bible doesn't say why they were taking so much salt, but we know that one of the reasons they needed it was to put on the sacrifices. They were anxious to begin the sacrifices again, that is why they had so much salt. Ezra 7:22 states: *"Unto an hundred talents of silver, and to an hundred measures of wheat, and to an hundred baths of wine, and to an hundred baths of oil, and salt without prescribing how much."*

A study of Judaism will definitely cause you to think salt every time you think offering. Although the offering of the ram of consecration in Exodus 29 is the only sacrifice of its kind in the Scripture, it is like all of the others in the respect that salt was there. Salt, or personal holiness, is always a part of every service and sacrifice we offer to the Lord. It is the salt of the covenant and a statute forever.

In the consecration of Aaron and his sons, the three different sacrifices have three different applications. The applications or typologies of these three sacrifices represent justification, sanctification, and consecration. The bullock is first, and it is for justification. The first ram is sanctification, and the last ram is the ram of consecration. These three works of divine grace in the believer are of utmost importance. Without sanctification, you really have nothing to consecrate. Without justification, you have absolutely nothing to sanctify.

We see this clearly in Romans 12:1, *"I beseech you therefore, brethren, by the mercies of God, that ye present your bodies a living sacrifice, holy, acceptable unto God, which is your reasonable service."* The mercies of God have to do with the bullock of justification, or the sin offering. This represents the imputed righteousness, or robe of righteousness, that is only given by the grace and mercies of the Lord. The sanctification is the part of the verse that states, *"holy and acceptable unto God."* This also is a result of the grace of God working in our lives as we obey Him. The presentation of that justified and sanctified sacrifice is the consecration. *"Present your bodies a living sacrifice."* There is the justification, sanctification, and consecration.

I am in no way making an effort to begin a new doctrine called "the third work of grace," but too often we

> *The sweetness of the third work of grace*

leave out the work of consecration. Its absence has created a horrible void in the body of Christ that has caused a display of wholesale immaturity and carnality. The body of Christ has certainly beheld enough "justification only" type teaching that produces worldliness and spiritual wimps. Likewise, we have beheld an abundance of legalistic bondage from the sanctified that have gotten "cranktified." The only antidote is holy, sweet consecration of our justified and sanctified lives. This produces the sweetness of loving service to the Lord without the promotion of self.

The Apostle Paul was well aware of the danger to those who advance in Christ, who are not conformed to the world, and who are transformed in their minds. He knew they would be tempted to be high minded and spiritually proud. He follows his call for total surrender with a warning in this area in Romans 12:3, *"For I say, through the grace given unto me, to every man that is among you, not to think of himself more highly than he ought to think; but to think soberly, according as God hath dealt to every man the measure of faith."* The Apostle Paul was very passionate in his call for holy consecration, using the words, "I beseech you," meaning "I beg you." Being a Jew, it is totally understandable that he would use terms relating to Judaism to call his fellow Christians to a deeper walk. He ached for them to be consecrated to the Lord. The apostles, prophets, evangelists, pastors, and teachers of our day should likewise beseech the body of Christ to be fully consecrated.

It seems paradoxical to say that the sweetness the church needs can only come through the salt of consecration, yet I believe that is correct. It is comparable to the concept of the great liberty of the Christian is only released as he becomes a slave to Christ. Being a bondservant to Christ produces the greatest liberty one could ever know. There are very few Christians who would not agree that there is a certain sweetness missing in the body of Christ today. It is that certain flavor of sweet holy consecration. We have sensed that flavor at times around those who are justified, sanctified and consecrated.

The consecration of the priesthood

Paul knew the devastation that would come to the Roman Christians unless they followed the sweet Holy Ghost into full consecration. Paul understood very well that as a born again Christian, he was a part of the New Covenant priesthood, even though he was of the tribe of Benjamin. He also understood and had studied many times the ceremony of the consecration of the priesthood. In his plea for consecration, he used terms that were conducive to that consecration service of Aaron and his sons in Exodus 29, because of the beauty of the typology and its absolute correlation to what he was preaching to the Romans.

Every sincere Jew would have been familiar with this consecration service because every priest of Judaism is connected to this service. In Exodus 29:1-9, we see the preparation for the consecration of the High Priest, "And this is the thing that thou shalt do unto them to hallow them, to minister unto me in the priest's office: Take one young bullock, and two rams without blemish, And unleavened bread, and cakes unleavened tempered with oil, and wafers unleavened anointed with oil: of wheaten flour shalt thou make them. And thou shalt put them into one basket, and bring them in the basket, with the bullock and the two rams. And Aaron and his sons thou shalt bring unto the door of the tabernacle of the congregation, and shalt wash them with water. And thou shalt take the garments, and put upon Aaron the coat, and the robe of the ephod, and the ephod, and the breastplate, and gird him with the curious girdle of the ephod: And thou shalt put the mitre upon his head, and put the holy crown upon the mitre. Then shalt thou take the anointing oil, and pour it upon his head, and anoint him. And thou shalt bring his sons, and put coats upon them. And thou shalt gird them with girdles, Aaron and his sons, and put the bonnets on them: and thou shalt consecrate Aaron and his sons." Their attire had already been given them in Exodus, Chapter 28. They had ornaments, beautiful clothing, bonnets and all manner of distinguishable accouterments that were all significant to the priesthood and certainly rich in typology. Aaron and his sons were then standing ready to be consecrated.

Notice the necessary provisions for the service: A bullock, two rams, a basket of unleavened bread, anointing oil, a crown with a mitre on it, and the attire of the priesthood. They were washed with water at the door of the tabernacle, and then they were dressed in their priestly attire. Everything was in order. The bull and the rams were without blemish. There was nothing lacking in preparation. All of Israel was waiting for one of the most important ordination services in the history of the world. All of the priests of Israel who will ever serve as priest at God's altar will be able to trace their ordination back to this very service. If they can't, they are not bonafide priests. There is absolutely no variance from this very important Levitical standard. This is very foundational to every sincere Jew.

> ***Every real priest of Israel
> must be able to trace
> their ordination back to the
> consecration of Aaron and his sons.***

THE SALT OF CONSECRATION

Actually, there was never meant to be anyone at the altar of the Lord in the entire Levitical order who had not been consecrated by the Aaronic priesthood. We see the reference to this in the battle between Abijah and Jeroboam in 2 Chronicles 13. When Abijah and his four hundred thousand men squared off against Jeroboam and his eight hundred thousand men, Abijah related to the salt covenant as the reason Jeroboam was going to lose the conflict. He also related to the fact that the camp of Jeroboam was full of false priests who had consecrated themselves. 2 Chronicles 13:9 says, *"Have ye not cast out the priests of the LORD, the sons of Aaron, and the Levites, and have made you priests after the manner of the nations of other lands? so that whosoever cometh to consecrate himself with a young bullock and seven rams, the same may be a priest of them that are no gods."* In other words, your priests have been ordained by men who are not able to trace their ordination back to Aaron's consecration. This was a major issue with all of Israel, and rightfully so.

We can see this mentality plainly in Judges 17. Micah, who was an idolater, had consecrated himself a priest for his idols, but when a Levite came by from Bethlehem-Judah, Micah hired him to be his priest. He consecrated the priest himself, which was forbidden, and thought this would bring blessing to his house. Judges 17:13 says, *"Then said Micah, Now know I that the LORD will do me good, seeing I have a Levite to my priest."* Of course, Micah was deceived. He had no right to consecrate a priest, but we can use his reasoning to prove our point.

Abijah knew his men were in the salt covenant and that the priests who were with him were consecrated, or he would have never made mention of Jeroboam's unauthorized priesthood.

Abijah understood the power of real consecration, and he also understood the devastation of false consecration. It is my steadfast belief that the real authority of every genuine Levite priest came from Aaron's consecration.

> ## *It all must begin with a sin offering.*

As we look further at the actual consecration service, we see that it begins with the offering of the bullock. We read in Exodus 29:10-14, *"And thou shalt cause a bullock to be brought before the tabernacle of the congregation: and Aaron and his sons shall put their hands upon the head of the bullock. And thou shalt kill the bullock before the LORD, by the door of the tabernacle of the congregation. And thou shalt take of the blood of the bullock, and put it upon the horns of the altar with thy finger, and pour all the blood beside the bottom of the altar. And thou shalt take all the fat that covereth the inwards, and the caul that is above the liver, and the two kidneys, and the fat that is upon them, and burn them upon the altar. But the flesh of the bullock, and his skin, and his dung, shalt thou burn with fire without the camp: it is a sin offering."* One could call this the bullock of justification because it is a sin offering. As we stated earlier, there is nothing to sanctify or consecrate unless it begins with the sin offering, or justification. We will see later in this chapter that the blood of the bullock was not applied to the garment of Aaron, as was the blood of the ram of consecration. The blood of the bullock was put on the altar and beside the altar for a sin offering. Then the fat and certain parts of the bullock were burned on the altar. The rest of the bullock was burned without the camp. This is so different from other sacrifices recorded in the books of the law, but very important in light of the fact that this is the beginning of the consecration service. It has to start with justification.

Of course, the blood on the altar is a type of the blood of Jesus on the mercy seat of the altar in heaven for the work of redemption and the justification of mankind to a holy God. The inward parts burned on the altar and the outer parts burned without the camp are a type of the vicarious suffering of Christ which enabled us to become priests unto the living God. The sin offering is a true type of atonement. Atonement is never to be confused with consecration or sanctification. Atonement is giving satisfaction for a wrong. Jesus is the atonement. He said, "*I am the bread*" or "*I Am*" is the bread. We have no part in the atonement, nor can we ever have a part in the work of atonement.

> ## *There is no atonement in our consecration.*

It is easy to see why the term *second work of grace* could be offensive to many. If there is an insinuation that we, our personal holiness, our sanctification or our consecration has any part of atonement in it, then it is not only offensive to man but also to God. If a person using the term is saying that we, through the grace of God, have the power to enter into sanctification and consecration, then it is acceptable to all. This is a work of grace to the believer, but it is not a work of atonement. It is true that the atonement affords the whole process of Christian experience, but it is not true that we, through any act of obedience or servitude, produce any part of atonement. Jesus is the bread. If we don't eat the bread, we have no part with Him, even if we live strict, holy and separated lives. We are never the bread. That is why the consecration service of Aaron and his sons begins with the offering of the bullock, which is a sin offering, a type of justification through atonement. Once we are settled into the peace of God through justification, we are ready to offer the ram of sanctification.

> ### *After the bullock of justification comes the ram of sanctification.*

Notice the unique difference in this offering as compared to the bullock, or sin offering. We read in Exodus 29:15-18, *"Thou shalt also take one ram; and Aaron and his sons shall put their hands upon the head of the ram. And thou shalt slay the ram, and thou shalt take his blood, and sprinkle it round about upon the altar. And thou shalt cut the ram in pieces, and wash the inwards of him, and his legs, and put them unto his pieces, and unto his head. And thou shalt burn the whole ram upon the altar: it is a burnt offering unto the LORD: it is a sweet savour, an offering made by fire unto the LORD."* There is still blood in the offering of the ram of sanctification, but there is no mention of a sin offering. This is very significant in the fact that the blood of Jesus makes us a candidate for sanctification, but there is absolutely no atonement in sanctification.

The Bible does not teach sanctification for the believer as a step of redemption. It is often presented as such, sometimes by well meaning and well versed Christians. But there is no scriptural validation for such a doctrine. The verses used to promote sanctification as a step in atonement are verses that use the term *sanctification* synonymous with redemption. For example, Hebrews 10:10 states, *"By the which will we are sanctified through the offering of the body of Jesus Christ once for all."* In this Scripture, the term *sanctification* is plainly speaking of the redemption of a lost soul. The sanctification of Christians comes after the initial work of redemption, but it is not atoning.

We read in 1 Thessalonians 4:3-4, *"For this is the will of God, even your sanctification, that ye should abstain from fornication: That every one of you should know how to possess his vessel in sanctification and honour."* This is not the sin offering, but the ram of sanctification. I understand that the sanctification of the unbeliever is really redemption, or the making of one holy. In that is atonement. But the sanctification of one already redeemed is an offering by fire to the Lord and has no atonement in it.

Certainly everything we receive from the Lord is a work of grace, and to number them offers no harm to the body. The terminology *first work of grace, second work of grace,* or third or fourth is neither wrong nor harmful in itself. It is harmful, however, to promote any experience that Christians might have as a step in their atonement. Again, we must learn from our Messianic Jewish friends the difference between a sin offering and an offering made by fire. The bullock was a sin offering, but this ram deals with sanctification of the priesthood, a burnt offering.

> *The ram of sanctification
> had its inwards washed.*

Notice the somewhat strange procedure involved in the

offering of this ram: *"And thou shalt cut the ram in pieces, and wash the inwards of him."* There is no other sacrifice like this in the Scripture, and this is the most important ordination service in the Jewish religion. Judaism cannot operate without a priest, and priests in Judaism have to trace their ordination back to this service. It is at this service that we find this unique offering. The ram is cut in pieces, and the inward parts are washed. This is exactly what real sanctification for the believer does. The Lord takes us apart limb by limb, and then washes us where we can not wash ourselves. This is that weapon that is not carnal which brings into captivity every thought to the obedience of Christ. This washing of the inwards is the sanctifying work the believer can experience. This is the renewing of the mind that Paul talks about in Romans 12:2, *"And be not conformed to this world: but be ye transformed by the renewing of your mind, that ye may prove what is that good, and acceptable, and perfect, will of God."*

This process is very important for the New Testament priesthood. The living sacrifice has to reckon itself dead in order to allow the washing of the inside. It would be a horrible sight to try to wash the inwards while the ram is still alive. Such an effort would display nothing short of madness. Yet, it resembles the futile efforts of some supporters of sanctification who try to wash their own inwards, without the death to the things of the world. The tearing apart of the sacrifice limb by limb is only painless to us when we are dead. Death to self is what the Lord is trying to accomplish in us. We have had a generation of teaching on how to live. The Holy Ghost really wants to teach us to die.

Notice after the ram was cut apart and the inwards were washed, the parts were all put back together. Evidently, the parts were all laid together in order with the head of the ram, and then the whole ram was burned: *"And put them unto his pieces, and unto his head. And thou shalt burn the whole ram upon the altar: it is a burnt offering unto the Lord."* This is the real fire of the Lord that sanctifies and purges the sacrifice. I hear a lot of people praying for the fire of God when they have no inclination at all toward sanctification. The thought of having their limbs taken apart, their inwards washed, being reassembled by the Lord Himself and then burned until they are consumed with God's fire does not seem to be their desire. The salt was certainly there on this ram of sanctification, and the beauty of this service sets the standard by typology for all the priests of the New Covenant priesthood. This is the ceremony the Lord set in order for them to begin their ministry. The ram with the salt on it was burned up with God's fire.

> ## *The dark powers despise the work of true sanctification.*

There is a lot of self-deception and guile in the area of sanctification. The devils fear biblical sanctification and consecration. I have often noticed an increase in the level of warfare when I minister to the body on this subject. Satan works overtime to try to mess up the salt. The reason he fears the salt covenant is because he knows the effectiveness of those who walk in this covenant. He tries to promote to the body of Christ a substitute or a compromise. The devil is fairly well pleased with ministers who preach and teach a light, almost entertaining experience and call it spiritual fullness. The devil is also pleased with holiness teaching that only deals with outward matters.

This ram of sanctification follows the bullock of justification to ever remind us of the preparation of the priesthood for service. I believe the dear Lord is speaking very strongly to His New Covenant priesthood in this hour about this matter. The flesh hates it. The world ridicules it. The church, for the most part, either denies it or is ignorant of it. It is deep. It is profound. But there is a renewing of the mind for Christians. There is a genuine work of sanctification after justification. The sweet Holy Spirit desires to do this great work in every believer, preparing us for the glorious realm of consecration.

> ## *The ram of consecration*
> ## *is now ready to be offered.*

As we go back to Aaron's ordination service, we will notice that the next ram is now ready to be offered. It is the ram of consecration. Again, we must remember that it is preceded by the bullock of justification and the ram of sanctification. We read about this offering in Exodus 29:19-22, *"And thou shalt take the other ram; and Aaron and his sons shall put their hands upon the head of the ram. Then shalt thou kill the ram, and take of his blood, and put it upon the tip of the right ear of Aaron, and upon the tip of the right ear of his sons, and upon the thumb of their right hand, and upon the great toe of their right foot, and sprinkle the blood upon the altar round about. And thou shalt take of the blood that is upon the altar, and of the anointing oil, and sprinkle it upon Aaron, and upon his garments, and upon his sons, and upon the garments of his sons with him: and he shall be hallowed, and his garments, and his sons, and his sons' garments with him. Also, thou shalt take of the ram the fat and the rump, and the fat that covereth the inwards, and the caul above the liver, and the two kidneys, and the fat that is upon them, and the right shoulder; for it is a ram of consecration."*

This is a most intriguing service. The strange use of the blood of this ram is very important in understanding the salt of consecration. Notice that first of all the blood was applied to their right ears. In the Old Testament, a hole was bored in the right ear of the slave who decided to stay with his master, even though he was free to go. (See Deuteronomy 15:16-17) This free slave is a true picture of consecration. As mentioned earlier, the greatest liberty in Jesus is found in being his bondservant voluntarily. Paul said in 1 Corinthians 6:12, *"All things are lawful unto me, but all things are not expedient: all things are lawful for me, but I will not be brought under the power of any."* Paul was free, but he chose to cancel his own freedom to be expedient for the body. This is a result of consecration to the Lord. It is a wonderful place to live.

The next thing they did in the ordination service was to put the blood of the ram on the right thumb of Aaron and his sons. I believe this is to signify the power to grip the things of God. They were being consecrated into the office of the priesthood. Their hands were to hold the things of the Lord, and they needed their thumbs consecrated. Down through the years, I have noticed the ability of people who walk in the salt covenant to hold on to the things of God and to grip the wonderful Word when it is given them.

> # *Consecration is a key to holding on to the things of God.*

There was an old preacher in our area who would often use the term *eternalize*. He would say, "You can't get it and keep it unless it is eternalized in your soul." When it comes to gripping the things of God, consecration is an important key. We need our thumbs sprinkled with blood so that everything we grip from God will come through the cross.

In each sacrifice of the consecration service, there is blood, even though the bullock was a sin offering. We are to constantly be reminded of the blood in every service we offer to the Lord. According to Revelation 12:11, we overcome the devil by the word of our testimony and the blood of the Lamb. Many quote that verse and stop short of the consecration found in the last part of the verse, *"And they loved not their lives unto the death."* This is an example of the need for the thumb to be consecrated. We need to grasp the whole counsel and hold onto it in the proper balance. Balance is exactly why the big toe of the right foot was also touched with the blood in this service. The great toe is for balance, and balance is a greatly needed commodity in the body of Christ.

After this part of the ceremony, Aaron and his sons had their garments sprinkled with blood and anointing oil. Exodus 29:21 says, *"And thou shalt take of the blood that is upon the altar, and of the anointing oil, and sprinkle it upon Aaron, and upon his garments, and upon his sons, and upon the garments of his sons with him: and he shall be hallowed, and his garments, and his sons, and his sons' garments with him."*

The Salt of Consecration

This is definitely an amazing service. Here stands the first high priest of Israel with his sons, in their complete priestly attire, dripping with blood from the altar, which is the blood of atonement and oil, a type of the Holy Ghost. Every priest who will ever serve in Judaism will be connected to this very moment. Every member of the New Covenant priesthood is also connected to this service through typology, the blood of Jesus for redemption and the power of the Holy Ghost to enable us to be the salt of personal holiness. The one thing left is the consecration of it all, or the presentation.

The wave offering

This consecration service is not over. The Lord gave them further instructions in Exodus 29:22-24, *"Also thou shalt take of the ram the fat and the rump, and the fat that covereth the inwards, and the caul above the liver, and the two kidneys, and the fat that is upon them, and the right shoulder; for it is a ram of consecration: And one loaf of bread, and one cake of oiled bread, and one wafer out of the basket of the unleavened bread that is before the LORD: And thou shalt put all in the hands of Aaron, and in the hands of his sons; and shalt wave them for a wave offering before the LORD."* There is the presentation of that which is redeemed and sanctified in the wave offering. The wave offering is always a representation of total surrender and a resigning of all of our rights and ambitions. Aaron and his sons have all of it in their hands now, including the bread of the offering. They wave everything in their hands to the Lord. This is the way of consecration. This is the beauty and the power of consecration.

It is so amazing that the Lord would require this kind of a service for the consecration of His first high priest to typify the wonderful work of redemption, sanctification, and consecration. Jesus, our great high priest from the tribe of Judah, after the order of Melchisedec, also had it all in His hands. In the garden of Gethsemane, He gave the wave offering when He said, *"not my will but thine be done."* He went on to suffer outside the camp and forever purchased our redemption with His own blood which He Himself placed on the mercy seat in Heaven. He has every right to call His royal priesthood of New Covenant believers to the wave offering of holy consecration.

After the wave offering, the ram and the bread were taken out of their hands and burned for a burnt offering. The breast of the offering was again waved before the Lord, and then given back to Aaron and his sons as a portion they could eat. Exodus 29:25-26 says, *"And thou shalt receive them of their hands, and burn them upon the altar for a burnt offering, for a sweet savour before the LORD: it is an offering made by fire unto the LORD. And thou shalt take the breast of the ram of Aaron's consecration, and wave it for a wave offering before the LORD: and it shall be thy part."* This consecration service is concluded with, I believe, the most powerful type of consecration yet. Aaron and his sons receive the choicest part of the sacrifice for meat. It is now his nourishment to sacrifice and give the wave offering. Jesus said it was His meat to do the will of the Father.

> *Consecration provides*
> *a great joy in sacrificing.*

THE SALT OF CONSECRATION

The deepest part of the glorious realm of consecration is when the cost no longer matters, when it becomes a great joy to pick up our cross, when we live to sacrifice and it becomes our meat to lay down our lives as living sacrifices. This is where the great Apostle Paul was walking when he said in 2 Corinthians 12:10, *"Therefore I take pleasure in infirmities, in reproaches, in necessities, in persecutions, in distresses for Christ's sake: for when I am weak, then am I strong."* Can you imagine this depth of consecration and devotion? There is not much talk of such consecrated service to the Master in our generation. Few are being challenged to such a lofty level of living on this side of Heaven. Yet, it is the standard that Jesus, our great high priest, gave to us. Jesus lived to do the will of His Father. It was His portion.

The Apostle Paul said with a passion born of sacred consecration in Philippians 3:10, *"That I may know Him, and the power of His resurrection, and the fellowship of His sufferings, being made conformable unto His death."* He was justified, sanctified, and consecrated to the Lord Jesus Christ. Consecration has no ability to redeem, but it is the goal of the Holy Ghost in the redeemed. We are called to sacrifice, with the full knowledge that in our sacrifice there is no sin offering or atonement. Our sacrifice is a burnt offering to the Lord. It is a sweet smelling savor to Him. We must never trust in our sacrifice for any part of redemption. We sacrifice only to please the Master.

The atonement enables us to follow Him where He went. He died, and we are called to die daily. He bore a cross, and we are called to pick up our cross. He suffered, and we are called to suffer for His great name. As the persecution of Christians around the world intensifies, the royal priesthood needs to get a good hold on the truth of holy consecration.

Walking in the Covenant of Salt

The salt of consecration is lacking to a great degree. It is the portion of the priesthood. It is the best portion, saved for the priests. It is *"the power of His resurrection and the fellowship of His sufferings."* Oh, the joy and bliss of full consecration!

The Lord went into great detail to institute the priesthood service of consecration for a very important reason. The bullock and the two rams are to forever typify to the New Covenant priesthood the way into the holy realm of the salt of consecration.

CHAPTER NINE

THE SALT OF OBEDIENCE

To walk in the salt covenant in this life is a lofty but attainable goal. So often Christians see things in the Bible, such as the covenants, and come to the sad, false conclusion that it is for someone else and they will never reach it. They have the revelation of it, but they can't seem to walk in it. I have said for some years now that the church in general needs much greater revelation in the things of God. This is true. But a greater need is for the church to walk in obedience to that which is already revealed. Many people stop the flow of the true revelation of the things of God by not walking in them. I believe this is a tremendous pitfall to many children of God. Deep revelation is given to the obedient child of God. Our failure to walk in what is revealed to us is often justified with great and extensive excusing ceremonies, but it is nothing more than disobedience.

Revelation demands responsibility, and responsibility is the fertile ground for receiving revelation. Much of modern Christianity is guilty of exalting revelation above obedience. This was totally unacceptable in the body of Christ just a generation ago. When revelation is exalted above obedience, there is a great problem. Knowledge, or revelation, is a snare without obedience. James 4:17 is a reference to this very circumstance, *"Therefore to him that knoweth to do good, and doeth it not, to him it is sin."* James is referring to him who has the knowledge or revelation but not the obedience.

Revelation demands responsibility.

It would be better not to have the revelation, than to have the revelation and not be obedient. We find a reference to this in 2 Peter 2:21: *"For it had been better for them not to have <u>known</u> the way of righteousness, than, after they have known it, to turn from the holy commandment delivered unto them."* It seems as if Christians today have the idea that the revelation of the matter is the end of it. I haven't heard anyone actually say such a thing, but I hear this concept in the conversations of the people of God. Ask Christians a question on the matter of fasting. Many will answer, "I know about fasting." Do you fast often? "I know about fasting." Obedience takes a back seat to revelation or knowledge.

I knew a lady who at one time visited the sick and ministered to those who were down and out. She would take her guitar and play and sing to those who were confined to their homes. After she got "deep" so to speak, her focus gradually changed from ministering to others to obtaining revelation. Obedience became secondary to her, and revelation became number one.

We have inherited a lot of this thinking from the humanistic teaching that has crept into the church. One of the proponents of secular humanism is the exaltation of knowledge without behavioral responsibility or obedience. From this comes the very real belief that education will solve the problem. For example, look at our nation's futile effort to stop venereal disease and teenage pregnancy by educating the children about sex. Statistics prove that more knowledge has not helped. It has actually made matters worse. This is because promiscuity is a behavioral problem. The behavior that produces the problem has to stop, and this requires obedience or behavioral responsibility.

Obedience is not even being emphasized in our pulpits, for the most part. It is revelation and knowledge that are being exalted and sought. This is why walking in the salt covenant (the salt walk) is so consequential to this last day outpouring. The salt covenant is the covenant of responsibility and obedience. Consider the wholesale madness of minimizing obedience, when the Bible teaches plainly that obedience is the condition of every promise of God. We can learn the power of this truth from our Messianic Jewish friends.

> ## *Obedience is the condition to all of God's promises.*

God said to the Jews in Deuteronomy 11:24, *"Every place whereon the soles of your feet shall tread shall be yours: from the wilderness and Lebanon, from the river, the river Euphrates, even unto the uttermost sea shall your coast be."* This is a powerful promise that the Lord gave to the children of Israel before they entered the Promised Land. We will discuss this promise later in more detail. It is one of the promises most referred to by the Jews today. Like all of the Lord's promises, it is either preceded by the condition of obedience or qualified later by it. The promise in verse 24 is preceded by the condition of the promise in verses 22 and 23: *"For if ye shall diligently keep all these commandments which I command you, to do them, to love the LORD your God, to walk in all his ways, and to cleave unto him; Then will the LORD drive out all these nations from before you, and ye shall possess greater nations and mightier than yourselves."* Israel has to deal with this truth every day. Obedience is the condition. Disobedience is the curse.

Walking in the covenant of salt will put an end to the light attitude toward disobedience in the body of Christ. One person said to me, "I am a child of God, just a disobedient child." I could see no remorse or grief over disobedience. There can be no salt in that person. Disobedience is always followed by deception. Deception is rampant in our society because of the exaltation of revelation above obedience. James 1:22 states, *"But be ye doers of the word, and not hearers only, deceiving your own selves."* Self-deception is the result of disobeying what we have heard or received by revelation.

We really have the doing (obeying) and the knowing (revelation) backwards. Jesus certainly didn't have them backwards. He said in John 7:17, *"If any man will <u>do</u> his will, he shall <u>know</u> of the doctrine, whether it be of God, or whether I speak of myself."* What Jesus is saying is totally different from this education worshipping society in which we live. Our society, including many evangelical churches, says, "If you know, then you can do." Jesus is saying, "If you do, then you can know."

> ## *God imparts revelation to the doers of His Word.*

Jesus taught that revelation comes to the doers of the Word. Discernment comes to those who obey and do. The dear Lord will reveal more truths to the doers of His Word than anyone else. Why should He reveal great things to those who are not going to do His obvious will?   People come to me, as they do other ministers, and ask me to pray for them to find the will of the Lord for their lives. It occurred to me one day that most of them are not praying for the *what* of the will of God, but are praying for the *where* of the will of God. This is another example of the exaltation of revelation over obedience. They want to know <u>where</u> they are to go more than they want to know <u>what</u> they are to do. In talking with them about their prayer request, I often hear these words: "If I just knew where I am supposed to be." I have learned to instruct these souls to be obedient where they are now. I advise them to concentrate on the *what* of God's will and then the Lord will reveal to them the *where* of His will. It always works.

We in America send a lot of missionaries all over the world to be in the right *where* of the will of God, and many of them never do the right *what* of God's will. They would be much better off in the wrong *where* doing the right *what* than to be in the right *where* but doing the wrong *what*. The salt walk is a walk of obedience. As obedience increases, so does the revelation. As the revelation increases, then obedience is loftier and sweeter.

THE SALT OF OBEDIENCE

> ### *All Christian growth is through obedience.*

The salt of consecration is evident in the life of an obedient servant of the Lord. The author of the book of Hebrews is scolding his readers for not being able to hear the deep things of the Lord. He says in Hebrews 5:11-13, *"Of whom we have many things to say, and hard to be uttered, seeing ye are dull of hearing. For when for the time ye ought to be teachers, ye have need that one teach you again which be the first principles of the oracles of God; and are become such as have need of milk, and not of strong meat. For every one that useth milk is unskilful in the word of righteousness: for he is a babe."*

It is clear that the Hebrews were not growing in revelation. The natural response is to go after more revelation, especially after such a rebuke. The next verse, however, clearly shows them the reason they are so weak in revelation. They were going about it the wrong way, so the Word of God tells them how to grow right and who can handle the strong meat of the Word. We read in verse 14, *"But strong meat belongeth to them that are of full age, even those who by reason of use have their senses exercised to discern both good and evil."* It is evident by this verse that the writer of Hebrews understood that knowledge or discernment comes from doing the obvious will of God. The phrase *"by reason of use"* tells them that using what they have and being obedient to what they know will result in great discernment and revelation.

There are things we have to be led to do before we will know how to obey. However, the obvious and the written will of God requires nothing but obedience. When people tell me they are waiting until the Lord leads them to tithe, I ask them why not begin tithing because the Bible says to do this and continue to tithe until the Lord reveals to them they should stop. We don't need revelation to do the obvious will of God. When we do the obvious will of God He will reveal much more of His hidden will to us—more than we ever dreamed. There is no deep mystical aspect in the matter of obedience. It is simply obeying God and keeping His commandments because we love Him.

I received a call from a sincere Christian lady who asked if I could tell her what to do to stop lying. I understood that the lady was in deep guilt and shame over her sin. Her request sounded pitiful, and I really had compassion for her; and I did know exactly what she should do to stop lying. I realized that my response would probably not be well received and would most likely be considered a gross over-simplification. However, I told her what to do. I said, "Always tell the truth, and you will never lie again." I was not trying to be taunting, sarcastic or cruel. I was giving her the simple truth. She was looking for some bit of knowledge that would somehow cause her to automatically obey. She was expecting knowledge or revelation to change her rather than obedience to God's Word. As expected, my answer was not appreciated, at least not at that moment.

> *Often blessing is exalted*
> *above obedience.*

Another area in which obedience often takes a back seat is in the region of blessing. I am referring to the constant seeking of blessing instead of simple obedience to the obvious will of God. This problem has caused our nation to be dotted with what I call, "Bless me Jesus clubs." These groups are not in the salt walk because their focus is not on obedience, but blessing. I am afraid the blessing they will have to settle for will be something from the realm of emotions instead of the genuine work of the Holy Ghost. The Lord honors obedience. According to 1 Samuel 15:22, He prefers obedience to sacrifice and offering.

An example of the "Bless me Jesus" syndrome is Christians who drive for hundreds of miles to stand in line for a blessing from one of their favorite preachers. They pass through poverty stricken, spiritually dark, and troubled areas to get to their destination. They didn't consider these hurting people on their way in, and they didn't seek a blessing in order to help them on the way out. People who are focused on blessings can be very cruel. They run from place to place to get their blessings because they never enter into the real blessing of the Lord. They are driven to seek revelation and blessing, but they do not seek to have the salt walk of surrendered and yielded obedience. True blessing evades them because they have by-passed obedience.

> ## *We have exalted "faith" above obedience*

Another error I have noticed in the body is the exaltation of faith above obedience. No one would think of saying to the body of Christ that their faith exempts them from obedience. Yet the constant exaltation of faith without reference to obedience and personal holiness brings the same results as if they were openly speaking this. We know that without faith we cannot please God. This is fundamental. However, faith to move mountains does not lift us above obedience. This problem, for the most part, has developed and magnified in the last fifty years. Books, songs and sermons written or preached before 1950 on the subject of obedience and personal holiness would far outnumber those on faith. Since 1950, the sermons, songs and books on faith will far outnumber those on obedience. This occurrence has caused the church in general to talk a lot about something that isn't really working for them. Genuine working faith has been negated by a lack of obedience.

One of the favorite old hymns written by one walking in the salt covenant is *"Trust and Obey."* It was written by Dr. Daniel B. Towner of Chicago. Dr. Towner worked in the music department for Dwight L. Moody. In 1887 a young man from Brockton, Massachusetts was stirred by a message delivered by Brother Moody and came to an altar of prayer to unreservedly offer himself to the Lord's service. His testimony was, "I am not quite sure how, but I am going to trust and I am going to obey." Dr. Towner, after hearing the young man's sincere testimony, immediately formed the chorus in his mind, "Trust and obey, for there's no other way, to be happy in Jesus, but to trust and obey." Every verse of that song is a tremendous testimony of the glory that falls on the life of obedience in faith. Verse four sums it up, "Then in fellowship sweet, we will sit at His feet, or we'll walk by His side in the way. What he says we will do, where he sends we will go. Never fear, only trust and obey." Faith must work with obedience.

See how the great Apostle Paul looked at this subject in Romans 1:5, *"By whom we have received grace and apostleship, for obedience to the faith among all nations, for his name:"* Here in this verse lies a secret of Paul's tremendous balance, *"obedience to the faith."* We see it again even more clearly in Romans 16:25-26, *"Now to him that is of power to stablish you according to my gospel, and the preaching of Jesus Christ, according to the revelation of the mystery, which was kept secret since the world began, But now is made manifest, and by the scriptures of the prophets, according to the commandment of the everlasting God, made known to all nations for the obedience of faith."* This glorious testimony of the great Apostle should forever settle the matter of exalting faith over obedience. I am not making an effort to minimize faith. I am making an effort to lift obedience again to its rightful biblical position.

Years ago, I went out witnessing and soul winning with a man who is now one of the elders at the church I pastor. We ran into a few brick walls, but we were trying to be obedient and do the obvious will of God found in the great commission. After our return to his house, we sat on his patio and discussed the things of the evening. We decided to pray for the power of the Holy Ghost so we could be effective in our witnessing. I will never forget that evening as long as I live. At that time, we had no idea of the significance of the direction we were approaching the Lord for this power. We had been out doing the obvious will of God, so we came to the revelation of our need. Faith swelled up in us to ask the Lord for the power of the Holy Ghost so we could better obey His great commission.

I remember my brother praying earnestly for the power of the Holy Ghost for soul winning. The last plea I heard him make to the Lord was, "I need this power to be a witness for the Lord Jesus." His prayer was interrupted by a glorious visitation of the Lord Himself. We were pinned to the concrete floor of that patio by the awesome presence of the Lord. We couldn't get up, and we didn't want to get up. The dear Lord poured into us His anointing and glory. Neither of us has been the same since that time. Our request was offered to the Lord in faith and obedience. It all lined up with the heart of the Lord, and He honored it.

Real faith is not polly parroting something we heard on a tape or read in a book. It is forever connected to obedience. It swells up in the heart of the one who abides in Him. Andrew Murray said, "He cannot with His Spirit make an abiding home in the heart of one who does not surrender himself utterly to a life of obedience."

> *We have even exalted worship above obedience.*

Another area where we frequently notice obedience being slighted is in worship and praise. Please understand that I am in no way minimizing worship and praise. I realize it is very dear to the heart of God. He inhabits the praises of His people. (See Psalm 22:3). True and genuine worship should be the occupation of every believer. It is the duty and the privilege of every Christian to worship and praise the Lord. But it is often exalted above obedience. You will never worship your way around the issue of obedience. It is total futility to try. The Lord loves it when we worship Him. But He loves it most when it comes from an individual with an obedient heart.

The salt of obedience on the sacrifice is a sweet smelling savor unto the Lord. When one has trusted the blood of the Lord Jesus Christ as his one and only sin offering, his obedience to the Lord becomes his burnt offering. The Lord loves worship with sweet smelling burnt offerings, with the salt of obedience. When we offer ourselves unto the Lord in sweet humble obedience, our worship rises to the Lord as a sweet, sweet savor. Away with lip service! (The lovely Savior deserves the worship and praise offered up to Him, and it should come out of a heart that He owns.) Jesus talked about a vain type of worship in some of His own people. He said in Matthew 15:8-9, *"This people draweth nigh unto me with their mouth, and honoureth me with their lips; but their heart is far from me. But in vain they do worship me, teaching for doctrines the commandments of men."* They disobeyed God and negated their worship.

If an estimable father had two sons, one who walked in integrity and one who walked in rebellion, from which would he most enjoy admiration and praise? Of course, he would enjoy the admiration and praise of the obedient son, rather than the rebel. Yet, in the body of Christ, there is a thousand times more emphasis on worship than obedience. I believe in public worship and private worship. It is wonderful. But without obedience, of what benefit are worship and praise to a holy God? This is like offering a sacrifice to the Lord without salt on it, or with salt that has lost its savor. It is good for nothing.

The Bible gives us the standard for worship in Psalm 29:2, *"Give unto the LORD the glory due unto his name; worship the LORD in the beauty of holiness."* Jesus said in John 4:23-24, *"But the hour cometh, and now is, when the true worshippers shall worship the Father in spirit and in truth: for the Father seeketh such to worship him. God is a Spirit: and they that worship him must worship him in spirit and in truth.*" Many Christians worship, or at least say they are worshipping, to see what they can get out of it for themselves. Some come close to worshipping worship. We do get something out of it, but that should not be our motivation for worship.

When obedience is exalted to its rightful biblical place, the worship will be a sweet savor unto the Lord. Holy communion will take place, and the Lord will be pleased. Worship from one who is walking in the covenant of salt is so beautiful. The Lord is pleased when we are trusting nothing but the blood of Jesus for our atonement. He is pleased when out of a heart of gratitude, we are obedient to every Word of God as salt on the offering. Worshipping in that sphere pleases the Lord greatly. When we are pleased because He is pleased, that is the true pleasure of benevolent worship. Such worship is with no other motive but to please Him. It is worship from an obedient heart.

The exaltation of promises above the commandments is also an indication of a low view of obedience in the body. A person with an obedient heart will not travel through the Word just looking for promises to cling to and act upon. I am glad for all the promises, and I have certainly found them sweet to my soul. But His commandments ought to be just as precious to us as His promises. The exaltation of promises above commands is common in the body of Christ.

> *God's commandments ought to be as precious to His children as His promises.*

THE SALT OF OBEDIENCE

Listen to David, a man after the heart of the Lord. He says in Psalm 19:7-11, *"The law of the LORD is perfect, converting the soul: the testimony of the LORD is sure, making wise the simple. The statutes of the LORD are right, rejoicing the heart: the commandment of the LORD is pure, enlightening the eyes. The fear of the LORD is clean, enduring for ever: the judgments of the LORD are true and righteous altogether. More to be desired are they than gold, yea, than much fine gold: sweeter also than honey and the honeycomb. Moreover by them is thy servant warned: and in keeping of them there is great reward."* It is evident that David loved the commandments of the Lord very much. He esteemed them higher than gold and sweeter than honey.

Many Christians exalt the promises and endure the commandments. The salt of obedience can actually allow you to love the commandments with the same passion that you love His promises. When you reach this level, you are not far from the heart of God. A disobedient soul can not love the commandments of the Lord like he should. I firmly believe that when the church starts walking in the salt covenant, it will lift the matter of obedience from where we have trampled it back to its rightful lofty position.

In the matter of deliverance from dark powers or spiritual warfare, we can see the same problem. There is no question that deliverance from demonic power is a valid work of the ministry. Jesus spent about one third of His ministry delivering people from the power of the devil. However, Jesus constantly taught those to whom He ministered the importance of being obedient. He delivered the woman who was caught in adultery from a religious mob and from her sin, but He told her to *"go and sin no more."* It is very dangerous to exalt the ministry of deliverance without emphasizing obedience. Can you imagine disobedient children of God screaming at demons and commanding them to do this and that? The demons laugh and mock at them. They know and understand who really has power over them.

> *Most genuine deliverance*
> *comes through simple obedience.*

It is so sad to hear people who aren't even walking with the Lord in holiness boasting of their power over the dark world. I have heard many discourses about our power over the devil, with no mention of the salt of personal righteousness. The dark world has a picnic when worldlings try to deal with them. Peter talked about these so-called ministers who promise freedom and deliverance to their listeners, when they themselves are bound with sin. 2 Peter 2:19 says, *"While they promise them liberty, they themselves are the servants of corruption: for of whom a man is overcome, of the same is he brought in bondage."* The simple fact is that spiritual bondage is a result of disobedience.

The Bible clearly teaches that the enemy comes in when the children of God disobey. This becomes very clear to us when we look at the history of Israel. When Israel disobeyed the Lord, He gave them over to their enemies. Every Jew understands this principal—disobey God, and your enemies will come in and rule you. People in bondage are trying to set others free from bondage! Jesus plainly taught that we should get our own eyes clean before we even help our brother get his clean, much less do warfare with the devils of hell.

The shortage of ministers walking in the salt covenant

is appalling. Genuine, true deliverance comes as a result of repentance and holiness. The Lord delivers those who repent of their sins and renounce the world and its ways. He constantly delivers His children who are walking in holiness. Consider the great verse of Psalm 34:19, *"Many are the afflictions of the righteous: but the LORD delivereth him out of them all."* It is plain that even the obedient or righteous need deliverance, but the promise is sure. He will deliver the righteous. 2 Corinthians 1:10 also deals with this subject, *"Who delivered us from so great a death, and doth deliver: in whom we trust that he will yet deliver us."*

It is not a false conclusion to say that He will not deliver the ungodly or disobedient. It is true that the Lord from time to time will deliver disobedient people if they have an intercessor who is righteous. We see this in the case of Abraham and Lot. Abraham prayed for Lot, and the Lord delivered Him from Sodom. All of us were delivered undeservedly from the grip of the devil through the righteousness of the Lord. It was the obedience of Jesus that set us free. Romans 5:19 states, *"For as by one man's disobedience many were made sinners, so by the obedience of one shall many be made righteous."* How can anyone separate deliverance and obedience?

In 2 Chronicles, Chapter 13, Abijah was delivered from the hand of Jeroboam by the covenant of salt. When he described his righteous stand to Jeroboam, Abijah made several references to the fact that the people in his camp were obedient to the Lord. They had the salt of obedience, and the Lord always honors that. They had praise. They had worship. They had the blessing of the Lord. They had the revelation, but they also had that salt of obedience.

WALKING IN THE COVENANT OF SALT

> ## *The Lord gives Israel four incentives*
> ## *to obey Him in the Promised Land.*
> ## *He loves to reward the obedient.*

We see the Lord calling for the salt of obedience in Deuteronomy, Chapter 11, as He is preparing the children of Israel to go into the Promised Land. This entire chapter is calling the Israelites to servitude, with incentives for obedience to the Lord. In this chapter, we can plainly see four incentives for obedience that will give us the salt to go on the sacrifice.

The first incentive is God telling Israel to obey Him in the land they are going to inherit because of the great things they have seen, or because of the greatness of the Lord. This is set forth in Deuteronomy 11: 1-7: *"Therefore thou shalt love the LORD thy God, and keep his charge, and his statutes, and his judgments, and his commandments, alway. And know ye this day: for I speak not with your children which have not known, and which have not seen the chastisement of the LORD your God, his greatness, his mighty hand, and his stretched out arm, And his miracles, and his acts, which he did in the midst of Egypt unto Pharaoh the king of Egypt, and unto all his land; And what he did unto the army of Egypt, unto their horses, and to their chariots; how he made the water of the Red Sea to overflow them as they pursued after you, and how the LORD hath destroyed them unto this day; And what he did unto you in the wilderness, until ye came into this place; And what he did unto Dathan and Abiram, the sons of Eliab, the son of Reuben: how the earth opened her mouth, and swallowed them up, and their households, and their tents, and all the substance that was in their possession, in the midst of all Israel: But your eyes have seen all the great acts of the LORD which he did."* What a lofty incentive to obey the Lord's commandments! Because He is a great and awesome God, it behooves us to obey Him. The Lord is rehearsing some of His wonderful acts to the children of Israel. He is saying to them, "You know how mighty I am. You saw my mighty hand. You know how I fought for you. Now keep my commandments in the land I am giving you." The highest incentive for obedience is to obey Him because of His greatness.

God gives Israel a second incentive for obedience. He tells them they ought to obey Him simply because He told them to. He says in Deuteronomy 11:8, *"Therefore shall ye keep all the commandments which I command you this day..."* This is also a high and lofty incentive for obedience. It is so pleasing to the Lord when we obey Him simply because He told us to, without feeling a tingle, without a prophecy, without a secondary motive, and without reservation. Simple and plain obedience demonstrates His lordship over our lives.

This was Paul's description of the God of Heaven that spoke to him on the ship in the storm in Acts 27:23, *"For there stood by me this night the angel of God, whose I am, and whom I serve."* Paul is saying, "He owns me, and I serve Him. I belong to Him through the atonement, and I serve him to demonstrate His lordship." Actually, here is a good New Testament description of the covenant of salt. He owns me. He bought me with His blood. That is bread. I am serving Him. I am obedient to Him. Obeying Him because He said so is the salt of obedience.

Israel's third incentive to obey God is because it is the best thing for them. The Lord says in Deuteronomy 11:14-15,

WALKING IN THE COVENANT OF SALT

"That I will give you the rain of your land in his due season, the first rain and the latter rain, that thou mayest gather in thy corn, and thy wine, and thine oil. And I will send grass in thy fields for thy cattle, that thou mayest eat and be full." This is not the highest incentive for obedience, but it is definitely an incentive. The dear Lord demands obedience from His children. It is the way that we demonstrate our love for Him.

Jesus said in John 14:15, *"If you love me, keep my commandments."* However, He is telling the children of Israel to obey Him in this new land because it is the best thing for them. He wants them to know that their lives will be sweeter if they obey Him. He wouldn't have told them this if He hadn't known that sometimes we lose sight of the higher incentives and fall to this level. Our obedience is so important to Him that He allows us to use this lower incentive for obedience: it is the best thing for us.

In the fourth incentive, God tells them to obey Him because He will punish them if they don't. We find this in Deuteronomy 11:16-17, *"Take heed to yourselves, that your heart be not deceived, and ye turn aside, and serve other gods, and worship them; And then the LORD'S wrath be kindled against you, and he shut up the heaven, that there be no rain, and that the land yield not her fruit; and lest ye perish quickly from off the good land which the LORD giveth you."* This is the lowest incentive for obedience, but it is a good one. We are to fear the Lord and obey Him in awesome reverence.

God is a God of mercy, but He is also a God of judgment. The newest Bible student can easily see that the Lord will quickly judge and chasten His own. He deals with disobedience with a total benevolent love and justice. He speaks very plainly of this matter in Deuteronomy 11:26-28, *"Behold, I set before you this day a blessing and a curse; A blessing, if ye obey the commandments of the LORD your God, which I command you this day: And a curse, if ye will not obey the commandments of the LORD your God, but turn aside out of the way which I command you this day, to go after other gods, which ye have not known."*

> ## *The four incentives for obedience God gave Israel can be applied to every area of our Christian service.*

These four incentives for obedience were given to the children of Israel at a strategic time in their history, but they are important to all of God's children today. These incentives, in fact, pertain to everything the Lord wants us to do as service to Him. Consider any part of your duty as a Christian and place it in the light of these incentives for obedience which the Lord gave the children of Israel. It is easy to see the importance of this charge to obey. For example, the fundamental duty of a Christian is to study the Word of God. I should obey the Lord in this matter because of how great He is. His Word is wonderful and glorious! It is worthy of my attention and my study. I ought to study my Bible because He told me to do it in 2 Timothy 2:15, *"Study to show thyself approved unto God, a workman that needeth not to be ashamed, rightly dividing the word of truth."* I ought to study my Bible because it is the best thing for me. I will certainly profit from wallowing in the Word. I ought to study my Bible because if I don't, I will reap chastisement. I will be blown about with every wind of doctrine.

Why should I obey the Lord in tithing? I should tithe because of the greatness of the Lord, because God told me to, because it is the best thing for me, and because if I don't I am a robber of God and must be punished. We can apply these incentives to every aspect of our Christian service. The salt of personal righteousness can only exist in a life of obedience. These incentives start with the loftiest and end with the lowest, but they are given to us through the Jews as a great stimulus to obey God.

I would like to say that I always obey Him from that highest incentive, but the truth is that I sometimes slip to the very lowest incentive and obey Him because I fear His chastening hand. The Lord knew His children would need all four of these incentives in this land flowing with milk and honey. They are written for our admonition today. The Lord promised great things to His children if they would obey Him. The Lord has not changed. He still rewards obedience.

Look again at the strength of the promise of reward for obedience in Deuteronomy 11:22-25, *"For if ye shall diligently keep all these commandments which I command you, to do them, to love the LORD your God, to walk in all his ways, and to cleave unto him; Then will the LORD drive out all these nations from before you, and ye shall possess greater nations and mightier than yourselves. Every place whereon the soles of your feet shall tread shall be yours: from the wilderness and Lebanon, from the river, the river Euphrates, even unto the uttermost sea shall your coast be. There shall no man be able to stand before you: for the LORD your God shall lay the fear of you and the dread of you upon all the land that ye shall tread upon, as he hath said unto you."* These wonderful promises, like all of God's promises are conditional, and that condition is obedience.

> ### *The salt of obedience*
> ### *affords great benefits and rewards.*

Years ago, I had the privilege of preaching in the nation of Sierra Leone, West Africa. We were holding a tent meeting in a city of that nation called Moyamba. The Lord was really moving and several Muslims were being converted, including a lady who was Chieftain over a large number of people. It was exciting. Revival was in the air. We were set up on the campus of a Christian school operated by a mission group from the United States. The children of the school kept telling me about a certain teacher named Virginia. I could tell by the way they spoke of her that they had a great love and admiration for her.

After a few days of hearing about Virginia, I decided to go meet her for myself. I knocked on her door and she answered from another room. She said, "Just a minute" in a sweet and motherly tone that made me know she thought it was one of the children knocking at the door. When she came to the door, I saw a very clean, neat, attractive lady of late fifties who literally shone with anointing from the Lord.

While I was at the door, I remember thinking that I would probably need to minister to this tired, lonely missionary dwelling in the midst of such abject poverty. When I saw her countenance, I quickly realized that she was the one who needed to minister to this evangelist. We talked a few minutes, and I learned that she had been faithfully praying for the meetings each night. I asked how she got to Moyamba and how long she had been here. She told me that as a young lady, raised on a farm in Iowa, the Lord had moved mightily upon her life and gave her a yearning to do His work. She said, "I fell so in love with Jesus that I told Him I would go anywhere He said for me to go." She said, "I am here in obedience to what He told me to do and where He told me to go. I have been here 39 years, and I won't be leaving until He tells me to leave."

I have never met a more vibrant child of God than Virginia. Her salt of obedience made me thirsty. Hers is the kind of salt Jesus wants on His bread.